George Barna is a master at digging useful insights
out of his cutting edge research. He is both deeply
rooted in eternal truth and very pragmatic in
applying these truths for the 21st century.

BOB BUFORD, AUTHOR & FOUNDER
LEADERSHIP NETWORK

ATE DUE

In a time when leadership in ministry must be
clear and decisive, TURNING VISION INTO ACTION
is a valuable tool.

PHIL DOWNER, PRESIDENT
CHRISTIAN BUSINESS MEN'S COMMITTEE OF USA

This is not merely another of many books about vision
and leadership; it is a helpful book—one of few
that practically guides you in charting a path
into future ministry.

DR. LUDER G. WHITLOCK, JR., PRESIDENT
REFORMED THEOLOGICAL SEMINARY

TURNING
VISION
INTO
ACTION

GEORGE BARNA

Regal Books
A Division of Gospel Light
Ventura, California, U.S.A.

Published by Regal Books
A Division of Gospel Light
Ventura, California, U.S.A.
Printed in U.S.A.

Regal Books is a ministry of Gospel Light, an evangelical Christian publisher dedicated to serving the local church. We believe God's vision for Gospel Light is to provide church leaders with biblical, user-friendly materials that will help them evangelize, disciple and minister to children, youth and families.

It is our prayer that this Regal book will help you discover biblical truth for your own life and help you meet the needs of others. May God richly bless you.

For a free catalog of resources from Regal Books/Gospel Light please contact your Christian supplier or call 1-800-4-GOSPEL.

Library of Congress Cataloging-in-Publication Data
Barna, George.
    Turning vision into action / George Barna.
      p. cm.
    Includes bibliographical references (p.).
    ISBN 0-8307-1866-4 (trade paper)
    1. Clergy—Office. 2. Pastoral theology. 3. Christian leadership. 4. Vision. I. Title.
    BV660.2.B329 1996
    253—dc20
                               96-8076
                                  CIP

2 3 4 5 6 7 8 9 10 11 12 / 02 01 00 99 98 97

Rights for publishing this book in other languages are contracted by Gospel Literature International (GLINT). GLINT also provides technical help for the adaptation, translation and publishing of Bible study resources and books in scores of languages worldwide. For further information, contact GLINT, P.O. Box 4060, Ontario, CA 91761-1003, U.S.A., or the publisher.

Contents

Acknowledgments

Let me identify the cast of characters who have, in some way, influenced this book.

My friends and colleagues at Gospel Light/Regal Books have been very encouraging, patient and supportive—the company consists of more than 100 people. I do not know them all, but each person plays a role in developing, publishing, distributing and supporting a book such as this. My thanks to them all.

My special gratitude is devoted to Bill Greig Jr., Bill Greig III, Debbie Vargas, Kyle Duncan, Kim Bangs, Bill Denzel, Dennis Somers, Virginia Woodard, Gloria Moss and the field representatives who distribute this book into the hands of those who might profit from it.

My friends and colleagues at the Barna Research Group, as usual, endured my physical absence and my absent-minded presence during the time I wrote this book. Thanks, Kelli Urban, Pam Tucker, David Kinnaman, Russell Harrison, George Maupin and David Young. Now, they can hold me accountable to be the visionary leader of our joint ministry.

Many people helped me see and experience vision through their lives. I am indebted to Luder Whitlock, Ron Sider, Bob Buford, Bill Hybels, Tom Phillips and Jim Scott, to name a few. They are people whose vision-based transparency and whose depth of vision enabled me to identify key aspects of the visionary life, which I could then study more broadly. Each of them is a case study of someone who turned vision into action.

A small but mighty band of prayer champions also asked God to bless this project and my efforts in making it tangible. Thanks to Paul Cedar, Greg and Suzanne Edmonson, Tom and Laura Greanias, Cindy McMasters, Tom Phillips, Steve Russo and Jim and Molly Scott. They helped make the battle winnable.

As always, I reserve my most special expression of appreciation for my beloved family. My wife, Nancy, sacrificed much while this book was being written. I hope it is worthy of the time, energy and comforts she gave up during my hibernation.

Our children, Samantha and Corban, reluctantly but graciously allowed me time to think, pray and write; time when we could have been playing together. I pray that the influence of this book will justify their investment and that a tangible consequence will be a better world in which they may live as a result of Christians pursuing God's vision.

This book, like everything I do, has been significantly influenced by the lives of Nancy, Samantha and Corban. May it be a valued reflection of our family values in the service of God.

Reflections on Vision

"If your vision is for a year, plant wheat. If your vision is for a decade, plant trees. If your vision is for a lifetime, plant people." —Chinese Proverb

* * *

"Some things have got to be believed to be seen." —Ralph Hodgson

* * *

"Lord, grant that I may always desire more than I can accomplish." —Michelangelo

* * *

"The world hates change, yet it is the only thing that has brought progress." —Charles Kettering

* * *

"A poet was once asked: 'If your house was burning and you could save only one thing, what would you save?' The poet answered, 'I would save the fire, for without the fire we are nothing.'" —Anonymous

* * *

"Nothing worth doing is completed in our lifetime." —Reinhold Niebuhr

* * *

"Vision is the art of seeing things invisible." —Jonathan Swift

* * *

"The future is where our greatest leverage is." —Joel Barker

Proverbs 29:18

"Where there is no revelation, the people cast off restraint" (*NIV, NKJV*).

* * *

"Where there is no vision, the people perish" (*KJV*).

* * *

"Where there is no vision, the people are unrestrained" (*NASB*).

* * *

"Where there is no vision the people run wild" (*MLB*).

* * *

Ministry Without Vision Is Like...

- a cow loose in the pasture: just grazing;
- a glacier: fascinating to observe, but going nowhere fast;
- a snake: ill-focused, spineless and attracted to whatever is hot;
- a rabbit: warm and fuzzy but utterly defenseless;
- a movie set: merely a facade;
- a flashlight without batteries: willing but powerless;
- Russian roulette: a dangerous game;
- a woman proposing to Boy George: it won't change a thing;
- a wedding without a bride: missing an essential element;
- a cadaver: stiff, predictable and lacking a discernible heartbeat;
- Fred without Ginger, Ozzie without Harriet: incomplete;
- a car without gasoline: capable of forward movement, but lacking the necessary fuel;
- a symphony without a score: lots of talent, but no direction;
- a preacher who has not prepared the sermon: the intersection of arrogance and ignorance.

Preface

Four years ago I had the privilege of writing a book entitled *The Power of Vision*. If I am to believe the things people tell me and the mail that arrives at my office, it was a life-changing book for literally thousands of people.

It was the first time many of them had heard of, much less understood or implemented, vision. For others, the book clarified what had been a murky concept. For me, it was a special blessing to share my study and thoughts about that concept.

I have spent thousands of hours and thousands of dollars researching how business, ministry and leadership influence people. It has convinced me that vision is central to making a positive and lasting difference in the world. I am similarly persuaded that until members of the Christian Body in this country exercise their abilities to discern God's vision for their lives and ministries and then make wholehearted commitments to such vision, the Church will continue to struggle.

In *The Power of Vision*, I addressed many of the basic elements related to vision. Topics included (1) the definition of vision and its core components; (2) the relationship of vision to leadership; (3) the distinction between mission and vision; (4) misperceptions and myths that hinder a person or group from experiencing true vision; (5) the difference between human vision and vision from God; (6) the process of discerning God's vision; (7) the characteristics of God's vision; (8) the benefits of, and obstacles to grasping vision; and (9) the key means of articulating the vision. In a relatively short number of pages, the book plowed through a lot of ground.

So why write another book about vision?

New Questions Emerged

Since *The Power of Vision* was released, I have traveled across the country teaching about and assisting pastors and church leaders with vision. A recurring set of experiences encouraged me to develop this second book about vision.

One compelling influence was the realization that in my teaching and correspondence with church leaders, a common set of questions kept emerging, probably a couple of dozen questions in all. Perhaps you have wrestled with some of the same questions. For example:

- Can anyone be a visionary or is this the domain of unusually gifted and specially called people?
- Does vision require targeting a specific people group or demographic segment? Doesn't that conflict with Jesus' ministry of reaching out to everybody?
- Doesn't vision make a ministry too narrow?
- How do leaders integrate the vision for their corporate ministry (e.g., a church) with the vision for their personal ministry?
- How do you measure whether the vision has been fulfilled?
- Does the vision change if a church calls a new pastor?
- What can be done if a church does not have a visionary pastor?
- Can a church pursue an effective ministry if it has a sense of mission but does not have an articulated vision?
- How can a visionary persuade those people who resist the vision to embrace it?
- What if your personal vision for ministry differs from the vision articulated by your church? Should you stay and adapt, stay and fight, leave with a fuss or leave quietly?

- How long should you wait before developing a new vision?

The Power of Vision was, for many people, a conceptual book, and it served a vital purpose in communicating basic truths about a concept that had previously been ignored or misunderstood by many. After embracing the concept, many people were left searching for a resource that would help them convert vision into action. They wanted to make the concept practical; and that, of course, is the essence of vision. My hope is that this book adequately addresses these concerns.

New Lessons Learned

Another motivation for writing a second book about vision is that I have learned much about vision since the first book was published. Those lessons included:

- Individuals and churches that are content to operate solely on the basis of their mission in life generally flounder because their perspective is too broad, too ill-defined. Those that focus on their vision as marching orders have a much higher chance of success because they establish more realistic priorities and because they are more likely to be people-centered.

- Vision, which I will argue is something every human being is called to discern and to apply, is unnatural for most people. It is the playground of true leaders, but most people are circumstantial, not natural leaders. By circumstantial, I mean that they find themselves in unavoidable situations in which they must exert some level of leadership even though they may not have much ability or inclination to lead. Because everyone must address the pressures and expectations of visionary behavior, however, helping everyone come to grips with vision is important.

- At its core, vision is a style of thinking, a process of dealing with current and future reality. It is not, as many people consider, a program waiting to be implemented.

- Contrary to my initial beliefs, I have found—through further biblical exploration as well as more prolonged observation—that vision is not dumped in people's minds by God all at once, but is progressively revealed to them. This process of incremental revelation is, in itself, fascinating to study because of what it teaches us about God's love for, and protection of, us.

- When people struggle with vision, the best thing they can do is

13

to continue asking questions. Vision is revealed through extensive inquiry into every aspect of our experience. The deeper our explorations, the more likely we are to gain the context, the focus and the comprehension needed to discern true vision.

• Vision is not a solution to a current problem. Many churches I have studied embark on a vision quest after they hit the wall and are desperate enough to try anything. Vision is not a quick fix. It is a long-term solution to long-term opportunities. Vision is the perspective that will permit an individual or organization to exploit untapped possibilities.

These are some of the lessons that made this project more compelling. If *The Power of Vision* was the conceptual argument, I pray that *Turning Vision into Action* will be the hands-on manual for becoming a practicing visionary.

Back to the Well?

In spite of the good response to *The Power of Vision* and the seminar I have conducted throughout the nation about the topic, I still had some trepidation about writing what might be considered a *Son of Vision*. Would anyone want to read a sequel? After all, how often do you enjoy a movie only to be disappointed by the sequels? How many authors have written a riveting novel but have followed that masterpiece with a derivative or shallow bomb? How frequently do we have to relearn the principle that you can never relive a glorious past, whether a magical vacation in Hawaii, an intimate personal relationship that has been put aside for years or fond memories of the town where you grew up?

Indeed, during my conversations with people about vision and the resources they needed to harvest God's vision in their lives, it seemed clear that the breadth of people's expectations for a follow-up book about vision might be impossible to satisfy.

If *The Power of Vision* had been intended as one book in a series and had been deliberately written in that manner, that would be one thing. But creating a free-standing resource that had stood the test of time and practice for four years, then creating a new link—it was possible, but...

So I spent a lot of time thinking and praying about the notion. The executives at Regal Books were patient and supportive as I rejected their expressions of interest in a second volume. Eventually, though, my concerns were addressed through various means and ministry experiences.

What You'll Get

The heartbeat of this book is to underscore the centrality of vision in our lives and to support that heartbeat with practical steps and insights in becoming a visionary leader, whatever your stature or position in life might be.

These pages present answers to common questions I am asked about vision, and corrections to some of the mistaken impressions about vision. They also present reactions to some of the abuses and inconsistencies I have observed as God's people have tried to make His vision real in their personal and in their corporate ministries.

I will recount some of the stories that seem to awaken the hearts of some people and lift the veil from the eyes of others. I will try to push you beyond the edges of your current ministry capacity and will encourage you to grow in faith and obedience to God's vision for your life and ministry.

One of the most difficult challenges in writing this book was deciding how to balance the discussion of personal and corporate vision. As an individual, you ought to clarify God's vision for your life and ministry. Separately, each church or ministry needs to have its vision from God articulated and accepted by those who comprise the ministry.

Sometimes the principles and procedures pertinent to individuals and to ministries are exactly the same. At other times, however, the approach is necessarily different. My prayer is that God will use these new insights in positive, practical and productive ways in your life.

Realize, too, that although a truckload of books have been written about vision since the beginning of the 1990s, the vast majority were written by business leaders for people living in the corporate world.

This book is written by a Christian for Christians. It relies heavily on insights from Scripture, observations and research among churches, parachurch ministries and Christian individuals. It is irretractably related to a relationship with God as a central requirement in discerning and implementing the vision.

Business leaders may use these principles, but without a deep, intimate and personal relationship with Jesus Christ, the content of this book may be mysterious and confusing.

I love the work of Warren Bennis, Burt Nanus, Peter Senge, Charles Handy, Alvin Toffler, Tom Peters and a few of the other respected business gurus. They are brilliant thinkers and strategic analysts. They do their homework, have an abundance of useful experience and offer valuable advice regarding vision.

None of these writers, however, have acknowledged that vision, no matter how expansive or innovative, is destined to failure if it lacks God's blessing and His imprint. God is the only reasonable starting point in the vision process. Anything else is merely well-intentioned, but flawed, methodology.

Be a Doer as Well as a Reader

The Father of all creation has prepared you for such a time as this. It is an exciting and opportune moment in the course of human history and in the maturation of the United States. God is counting on you to rise to the occasion. He has designed and gifted you in a particular way, allowed you to have certain experiences and has provided you with opportunities that will contribute to the fulfillment of His heart's desires for His creation.

If you wonder whether you have discovered God's vision for your life or ministry, know that neither I nor anyone else can ever tell you with certainty if you have truly discerned God's specific vision. It is possible, however, to identify the character of such a vision and to ask you to test what you deem to be vision against the definitional attributes of His vision.

As you grasp the totality of His vision for your life, your ability to satisfy His desires for you and for His creation will be multiplied. Living the visionary life is exhilarating and challenging. It is personally fulfilling and it is spiritually glorifying to God. Without a vision from God, you will flounder. In the intense and diligent pursuit of His vision you will know the bounty and joy of His blessings.

Visionaries Who Shaped Your Life

"WHEN IT COMES TO THE FUTURE, THERE ARE
THREE KINDS OF PEOPLE: THOSE WHO LET IT
HAPPEN, THOSE WHO MAKE IT HAPPEN AND
THOSE WHO WONDER WHAT HAPPENED."
—JOHN RICHARDSON

The future doesn't just happen; it is created by visionary leaders. People of distinctive foresight and unflappable conviction literally create the future. They conceive ideas that represent fundamental changes. They carefully and strategically propose them to the public. They tirelessly nurture acceptance of their ideas, and they serve as relentless advocates for instituting them.

If you don't like American society these days, look back at the past half century and identify the visionary leaders who introduced the seminal cultural changes that describe the nature of our lives today.

Vision, you see, is a clear mental portrait of a preferable future. Those who possess the vision become its primary champion. Through the force of their vision, reality is changed forever.

Americans Focus on the Future

Americans, as much as any people on earth, are transfixed by the future. Millions of us focus upon what is to come. For the poor and oppressed, the future represents their hope for a better existence. For the young, the future constitutes the era when they can dictate how life will be lived. For scholars and researchers, the future is the period when predictions and projections are proven or disproven, facilitating refinement of their reflections and their craft. Evangelical Christians pine for the future because it will bring the second coming of Jesus Christ and the ultimate spiritual fulfillment for His followers.

As the axiom says, however, the future ain't what it used to be. Yesterday's future is today's present. Here's the key: If you don't like the cultural conditions of the day, the culprits are rarely contemporary politicians, renowned university professors, prestigious clergy or powerful CEOs of global corporations.

No, if you want to extend your gratitude for a particular aspect of contemporary life or to point a finger of blame or accusation at those responsible for the cultural malaise of the day, you must go back 20, 30, maybe even 40 years and identify the paradigm pioneers of that time. Many of the core aspects of life as we know it in the late 1990s are a result of the ideas, programs, systems and policies that were introduced, advocated or initially instituted several decades ago.

Change in the significant aspects of life takes time. The seeds of change that were planted and nurtured decades ago are just coming into full bloom today.

Changing Your World

You can probably remember who was most instrumental in leading you to the point of accepting Jesus Christ as your Savior. If you are married, you can probably recall the person who introduced you to your spouse. But have you ever identified the visionaries whose ideas and efforts have shaped your life today?

Let me demonstrate the power of visionary thinking and behavior by briefly highlighting the work of just eight visionaries of the second half of the twentieth century. Perhaps you have never heard of some or were unaware of the transformational influence of others.

Driven to Succeed
Realize that being a visionary is not synonymous with being well

known or revered. It simply indicates that the convictions and efforts of the person have significantly altered the ways many people conduct their lives, whether the visionary's influence is acknowledged or not, whether the outcome of the visionary's influence is for the best or for the worst.

These people are not merely innovators, entrepreneurs, opportunists or specialists. Nothing is wrong with being such a person, but these people are markedly different from visionaries. For instance, John Rockefeller, the founder of Standard Oil and the catalyst of the Rockefeller fortune, is considered by many to be the founder of the modern corporation.

Rockefeller was driven by the desire to expand his profits and his influence, not to create a superior world in which others might live and find fulfillment. His innovations were designed to skirt federal regulations or to produce efficiencies that would lead to greater profit margins. Although his ideas were creative and took a measure of vision, he was not the kind of social visionary on which I am focused.

Hugh Heffner is an example of an opportunist. The founder of *Playboy* magazine and its related enterprises, Heffner simply seized the moment and cashed in on windows of opportunity created by true visionaries. He had little vision beyond maximizing his pleasure and taking advantage of opportunities to live in comfort and to establish himself as the supreme hedonist.

One of the world's great entrepreneurs is Rupert Murdoch, the Australian-born media mogul who has since become an American citizen. Ironically, his decision to become a naturalized citizen was motivated by his entrepreneurial drive: Only as an American citizen could he legally maximize his media holdings in the United States and reap larger profits.

Murdoch's empire encompasses the 20th Century Fox movie studio, the Fox television network, the HarperCollins publishing conglomerate and major metropolitan newspapers and radio stations around the world. He also owns a host of magazines and the SkyOne satellite delivery system that supplies most of the world (outside the United States) with television programming.

Murdoch's forte, however, is in formulating brilliant business and financial strategies. He displays unusual vision for media development, but his vision relates to financial profitability through entrepreneurial thinking and behavior.

Specialists are those who present to us breakthroughs in their areas of expertise. Theirs is a technical vision based on exaggerated proficiency in their crafts.

George Lucas, the brains behind the visual wizardry created at his

Industrial Light and Magic film production company, is such a specialist. Do the special effects he originated for trailblazing movies such as the *Star Wars* trilogy or *Jurassic Park* merit him the title of visionary? No.

Lucas is responsible for some astounding innovations within his area of production, but like all specialists, his vision is confined to technical processes or systems. It does not directly relate to creating a superior human environment or condition.

Let me introduce you to eight visionaries whose lifework has greatly influenced your life.

Alfred Kinsey

Perhaps it was inevitable that a man who began each day with a cold shower would emerge as the person most directly responsible for the sexual revolution of the United States.

> ALFRED KINSEY ENVISIONED A BOLD NEW ERA OF SEXUAL FREEDOM IN AMERICA AS HE INTERVIEWED COLLEGE STUDENTS ABOUT THEIR SEXUAL EXPERIENCES, PRACTICES, APPETITES AND EXPECTATIONS.

Known to some as the "patron saint of sex," Kinsey was a Harvard-trained biologist who in 1938 was invited by Indiana University to teach a course about marriage. True to his scientific training, his first step was to search for data about the state of marriage and sexuality. To his astonishment, he found nothing beyond government statistics about rates of marriage and divorce, fertility rates and the like. These were sterile, almost meaningless figures to Kinsey. He was interested in what made people behave sexually. Apparently, nobody had previously invaded the world of sexual intimacy with objective research.

Kinsey envisioned a bold new era of sexual freedom in America as he began to conduct extensive interviews with college students about their sexual experiences, practices, appetites and expectations.

Kinsey saw himself as the one who could empower millions of people to find the kind of sexual fulfillment they had always desired but had never achieved. Using his survey data as the scientific basis for his cause, he would gain the ear of the media and the public.

Consequently, Kinsey became a crusader for sexual liberation. He and his team of researchers conducted thousands of extensive interviews about people's sexual lives.

Kinsey burst onto the national scene in 1948 when *Sexual Behavior in the Human Male* was published, followed four years later with *Sexual Behavior in the Human Female*. His first book took the nation by storm, selling 200,000 hardback copies in its first two months. Almost overnight, Kinsey was established as America's leading sex expert.

Unfortunately, most Americans did not realize that Kinsey's agenda was not to provide objective, helpful facts about sexuality, but to "sexually liberate" the nation. His data, collected in the guise of scientific rigor, were horrifically (and intentionally) unrepresentative of the national public that he claimed to describe. For instance, a large proportion of his sample of males were prison inmates and more than one-quarter of his male subjects had been convicted of sex offenses at some point in their lives.

Kinsey recklessly disregarded these problems. He drew the conclusions he wanted to promote. Some sources have suggested he manipulated the data from his already-skewed samples to arrive at the conclusions he desired. Similarly, his samples of females were invalid. Three-quarters of his female samples were college graduates at a time when just 13 percent of the nation's women had earned college degrees.

Social scientists were outraged at Kinsey's practices and were aghast at his conclusions—and the massive audience he generated for his work. His academic peers, however, missed the point. Kinsey never sought scientific validity, although he continually professed that his work met the highest of standards.

Kinsey's aim was to promote sexual freedom and experimentation to facilitate happiness. He promoted homosexuality, premarital sex and even extramarital sex with abandon. Astoundingly, some of his research, now nearly half a century old, is still used by groups (primarily the homosexual lobby) seeking to promote sexual freedom.

One social analyst offered what he considered praise of the sexologist. "If there had never been a Kinsey, I'd never have seen Jacqueline Bisset's breasts, or Jane Fonda's....If there had never been a Kinsey, there would have been no personals in the classified columns....Most of us would have gone to our graves believing only models or showgirls were these lovely flowers of meat under their clothes....Because what he did, what he did *really*, once we took it all in, was to democratize flesh."[1]

Indeed, Kinsey's public standing, academic credentials and fervor for his cause enabled him to lay the groundwork for a sexual revolu-

21

tion that has brought about unnerving consequences: widespread divorce, pervasive cohabitation, births outside of marriage, rampant adultery, public acceptance of erotic art, pornography and homosexuality and the demise of virginity.[2]

Benjamin Spock

Until the genteel doctor came along, parenting education was accomplished largely through word of mouth, assistance from one's nuclear family and occasional tips gleaned from doctors on how to best rear children.

That changed in 1946 when Spock, a pediatrician and a graduate of Yale and Columbia, introduced two generations of parents to a new approach to child rearing through his seminal publication *The Common Sense Book of Baby and Child Care*. One of the all-time best-selling books, translated into more than 30 languages, this encyclopedia for parenting radically altered the foundations of healthy and effective parenting. The chances are overwhelming that you, as well as most of the people who read this book, have been substantively affected by Spock's philosophy.

Prior to Spock's book, the conventional wisdom was that parents should intentionally and aggressively shape a child's behavior to enable the young person to achieve self-reliant independence as early as possible. Spock, based on the belief that a child was entitled to the same understanding, respect and emotional support desired by adults, advocated greater leniency and flexibility in rearing a youngster. He warned parents of the dangers of harsh, physical or excessive punishment.

His timing couldn't have been better. In the wake of America's extensive participation in World War II, millions of Americans focused on having a family. Tired of sacrifice and fear, they were in the mood for a gentler approach to life. America was eager to hear someone spin a philosophy that contained fewer rules and was less regimented.

Throughout the 1950s and '60s, Spock's book was the bible of parenting. Millions of copies sold each year; but when the nation erupted in violence and disarray in the late '60s, some people began to raise questions about how the younger generation had been reared.

Respected public leaders, such as Norman Vincent Peale, a religious icon, publicly scolded Spock for encouraging permissive parenting. Spock responded that he had been misunderstood; people were reading into his work practices that were not on the written pages. Demonstrating his genuine concern for the plight of infants, youngsters and families, Spock has since revised the book several times, attempting to emphasize the importance of every child's need for parental guidance and for parents to stand their ground when disciplining a child.

The damage, however, had been done. Tens of millions of parents, and many more children, already had been influenced by his early, authoritative stance about how to rear a child of good character.

Spock's emphasis upon shaping the will and emotional well-being of a child, rather than focusing upon a child's behavior and expectations, has influenced the baby boom generation immensely. Its rejection of traditions, of rules and of time-honored principles and moral truths may be traced to an upbringing in which authority and absolutes were consciously rejected.

Spock, alone, cannot bear the weight of such blame. Parents had to choose to adopt and to implement such advice. The legacy of a visionary is seen in a person's influence upon people's perspectives and behavior, and Spock's extensive influence is undeniable.

Expecting instant gratification without consequences, whether through adultery, drug use or white-collar crime, are just a few results of the vision cast by the well-intentioned doctor who sought to redefine the role, the practices and the measure of a good parent.[3]

John Dewey

What Spock was to parenting, John Dewey was to education. A professor at Columbia University, Dewey fathered a philosophy of education known as the Progressive Education Movement, or pragmatism. His ideas had greater power after his death in the early 1950s than during his lifetime. Those ideas continue to haunt us today.

Dissatisfied with the kind of educational experience students were receiving in the public schools, Dewey theorized and passionately promoted a new approach to. elementary school education. He believed that an education that de-emphasized textbooks and rote learning in favor of a child-centered environment geared to personal experience would substantially enhance a student's ability to learn vital principles.

In his primary work, *On Education*, Dewey argued that education is most effective when it is based on a humanistic orientation. He encouraged educators to facilitate free-form experimentation and unstructured experience to naturally grasp the concepts to be learned. Dewey suggested that independent inquiry, in which the student engages with the topic through hands-on learning rather than force-fed information, would enhance the student's ability to perceive, to understand and to retain the vital lessons.

In modern parlance, the student would grow because he or she would "own" the process and the information. Thus, an education based on learning by doing, rather than one of listening to and regurgitating lectures, would foster true knowledge and insight.[4]

Dewey was the darling of the liberal policy makers of the 1960s and '70s who introduced "educational reform" through experimental learning at the elementary and secondary levels. In harmony with Dewey's theories, efforts were made to create the school as a community, facilitating "education as living, not as preparation for living."

Although Dewey's concepts have fallen into disfavor among many teachers, the residue of his philosophy is felt by the millions of adults now in their 30s, 40s and 50s who were exposed to "alternative education."[5]

William Levitt

Did you know that the United States is in the midst of its third residential pattern? Early on, the United States was an agricultural nation, one that we would today characterize as "rural." When industrialization and an expanding, bureaucratic government provided an ever-broader range of public services, the United States became a predominantly urban nation. Today, the United States is a suburban country: The bulk of the nation's population, wealth, expertise and productive capacity reside just outside of the central city limits.

Do you know what enabled the mass exodus from the city to the suburbs to occur? Many factors converged, of course, but Bill Levitt was largely responsible.

Perhaps you have heard of Levittown, the fabled cookie-cutter communities in the Northeast that spawned a new industry of home builders and a new generation of home owners. Levitt, the builder behind the communities that he immodestly named after himself, innovated an entirely new approach to home construction, home financing and community development.

Aware of the mass production culture of the 1950s and the acute need for a massive influx of available homes, Levitt saw his opportunity to blend his desire to make loads of money with his dream of creating widespread access to "the American dream." After the war, the United States experienced a housing crisis. Marriages skyrocketed after GIs returned from the battlefront, and the fabled baby boom ensued. Supply did not keep up with demand, at least in the housing sector.

Despite the rapid increase in new families, the housing stock remained at a standstill. Newlyweds doubled up with their in-laws, when they could. Millions of people, however, lived in garages, sheds, barns and other quarters unsuitable for long-term habitation. The problems? Lack of financing for potential home buyers and the inability of developers to construct homes inexpensively and quickly.

Levitt's time had come. A successful custom-home builder in New York, he set into motion an idea he had been nurturing for years: "site fabrication."

In the early 1950s, while others experimented and failed with the notion of prefabricated homes, Levitt divided the home-building process into 26 distinct steps and hired teams that would specialize in completing a particular step. He then purchased huge lots of farm-land outside of cities where the property was inexpensive and plentiful, and sent in his team of specialists to do their appointed task—one team at a time. They repeated that operation on many adjoining plots before calling in the next team of specialists to apply their special skills. He solved the financing problem by convincing the federal government, through the FHA, to guarantee 100 percent loans made by banks to veterans.

Soon veterans were lined up, or placed their names on waiting lists, to purchase these identical, Cape Cod-style homes located in massive developments. Most people were willing to overlook the bland appearance of these neighborhoods in return for having their own homes, modern appliances, instant communities, safe neighborhoods and new schools. Paying no money down, they could have a brand new home for less than $7,000.

Levitt's concept took off as fast as his house sales did. Other home-building companies, captivated by his startling sales record, followed his lead in other markets across the nation. Before long, the United States was dotted with tract housing and the housing crisis was eliminated. More importantly, a new class of home owners was born and the creation of suburban infrastructure began. *Time* magazine featured a cover story about Levitt, citing his work as "a revolution within the housing industry."

That compliment, grandiose as it may seem, greatly underestimates the breadth of his influence. Levitt revolutionized more than the housing industry. The suburban reality we have today—wide streets, sewage treatment capabilities, relatively new public facilities, large indoor shopping malls, omnipresent strip malls, suburban sprawl, racially and economically segregated communities, a different quality of life from rural or urban areas, Protestant megachurches, industrial parks and so forth—can be attributed to his vision for establishing a viable, affordable nonurban America.[6]

Ray Kroc

Few people would have expected Ray Kroc to make it big. A high school dropout, he served in the army with platoon mate Walt Disney, then bounced around as a disk jockey, musician, real estate broker and salesman. In the mid-1950s, Kroc, who lived in Chicago, was paying the bills by selling milk shake machines to restaurants. During his sales trips, he kept hearing about the milk shake units being used by the McDonald brothers' restaurant in Southern California. Intrigued by the street buzz, he flew to the area to determine what was causing all the fuss among restaurant owners, soda fountain operators and dairy-bar managers from across the nation.

Kroc was unimpressed. The restaurant's building was unremarkable, the location nothing special. As Kroc sat in his rental car in the restaurant's parking lot, carefully watching the activity around him, he was struck by two facts: People kept coming and coming, and they seemed pleased with what they bought. His sales instincts would not let him ignore these inescapable observations.

Kroc spent the day talking to customers, walking around the grounds to observe what was happening and eventually meeting the owners. They explained the entire process to Kroc, who by this time realized he was on to something special. By the end of the following day, Kroc had talked the McDonald brothers into allowing him to open up additional McDonald's restaurants as part of their newly-inked partnership deal.

As any true visionary would, Kroc felt compelled to act on what he had witnessed during his reconnaissance trip. Matters were heavily weighted against the success of this venture. Here he was, at age 52, starting a new company alongside partners he barely knew and lacking the money needed to adequately sustain the start-up phase. Physically, he was in no shape for the challenge. He suffered from arthritis and diabetes and had long since lost his gall bladder and thyroid glands. His wife was horrified that he was leaving his secure job for some cockamamy hamburger joint, in partnership with two men halfway across the country who were not overly interested in expansion in the first place!

Kroc was not to be deterred. In his mind's eye he had seen the future, and it was spelled f-a-s-t f-o-o-d f-r-a-n-c-h-i-s-e-s.

Kroc has left a legacy of two major points of influence. One, of course, was his role in establishing the fast-food industry as a major force in our nation's—and, now, the world's—economy. In a society in which time has become the most carefully guarded resource, it is hard to determine whether it was the customers' needs to protect their time that created the acceptance of the fast-food industry, or whether the availability of fast food heightened people's perceived need to maximize their time. Today, it is a moot point. The golden arches stand as a symbol of what Kroc did for America: apply technological innovations to heighten our efficiency.

The other legacy Kroc bequeathed to us was perfecting the fran-

> RAY KROC ESTABLISHED THE FAST-FOOD INDUSTRY AS A MAJOR FORCE IN OUR NATION'S—AND, NOW, THE WORLD'S—ECONOMY [AND INTRODUCED FRANCHISING IN HIS VISION FOR THE MARKETPLACE].

chise concept. Many people before him had franchised their operations, such as Dairy Queen and Tastee-Freeze; but none had done so as successfully. He worked tirelessly to develop a franchise package containing a now-legendary set of requirements and restrictions that have enabled McDonald's to maintain four distinctives Kroc deemed nonnegotiable: courtesy, cleanliness, quality and service.

Kroc introduced other innovations to the franchise arrangements he offered: refusal to require that franchisers buy their supplies from McDonald's, uniformity of the operations, extensive operator training and a special land-leasing arrangement for each restaurant. Those were just savvy business decisions. The key was Kroc's vision for the potential of franchising.

Many other corporations entered the fast-food franchising field because of Kroc's profitable expansion efforts. None, however, can match the cumulative record of success enjoyed by the 7,500 McDonald's restaurants throughout the world.[7]

Earl Warren

It may seem odd to include a U.S. Supreme Court justice among the core visionaries of the last half century. Of all the justices to select, Earl Warren may seem to be an odd choice. This was the man appointed to the court by President Dwight Eisenhower, an appointment the president later said "was the biggest damn fool thing I ever did." Warren, however, low key and unassuming, fathered a legal and judicial revolution that still touches our lives today, several decades after his retirement and eventual death.

27

Warren initially pursued a common track for a law school graduate: private practice, district attorney and state attorney general. He then was elected as governor of California for three terms. A rising political star, he was the vice-presidential nominee of the Republican Party in 1948, but suffered his first political defeat when Thomas Dewey's campaign was unsuccessful.

After one term of Harry Truman's leadership, though, the nation elected the war hero Eisenhower as chief executive. In deference to Warren's support for Eisenhower's nomination, the president appointed Warren to the highest court. He did so expecting the Californian to be an ideological moderate with Republican leanings. How wrong he turned out to be.

Those who knew Warren found him hard to describe. Adjectives often included "bland," "nondescript," "pleasant," "innocuous" and "simple." He was considered a shrewd political tactician, but an ordinary intellect. As much as anything, he seemed to have the knack of being in the right place at the right time.

His closest friends, however, admitted that as Warren moved through the political system, they could see him slowly change. He became increasingly interested in applying fairness, equality and justice to all walks of life, a matter of fact rather than a matter of public policy debate.

During his 16 years on the bench, Warren masterminded a thicket of judicial precedents. He championed rulings that outlawed segregation, prohibited any form of racial discrimination, provided new rights and legal options for the poor, expanded freedom of speech, extended protections for freedom of the press and increased rights related to political dissent. His court practically rewrote the criminal justice code.

Through a dogged emphasis upon moral duty and fair play, Warren stretched the parameters of how activist the court could be in its rulings and how invasive the law could become in dictating right and wrong.

The legal and judicial standards we know today were largely shaped by Warren. He did not create the system, of course, but he envisioned the contours of a just and equality-based society that still define many of the limits and lifestyles that characterize America in the late 1990s.[8]

Martin Luther King Jr.

Americans have a tremendous penchant for forgetting their history. We quickly absorb major social changes and forget the sacrifices made by those who fought the battles.

I fear that the hard-won victories of Martin Luther King Jr. are among those that have been so blithely overlooked. Yet, King's influence will be crucial to fostering racial understanding and unity in our increasingly diverse population.

King, the son of a Baptist preacher, grew up in the South during the 1930s and '40s. Like every black living in the South, he was well acquainted with the varieties and manifestations of racism. Among the images etched indelibly upon his mind was the incident that occurred at age 6 when the parents of a white friend angrily interrupted their playtime and demanded that King never again play with their son. When he was 11, a white woman, without provocation, hit him and called him a "nigger."

Of course, these and many other incidents occurred in a context of injustice. Prior to the mid-'60s, blacks were not allowed to eat in white restaurants, to use public restrooms or to ride public transportation. The young King watched, listened and absorbed the pain; and he prepared to devote his life to the fight against social injustice, poverty and racial discrimination.

King was an intelligent man. He entered college at age 15 without completing high school, was ordained at his father's church at age 18, was valedictorian of his seminary class and earned a Ph.D. in theology from Boston University.

King then entered the school of hard knocks, pastoring a church in Montgomery, Alabama. Using his pulpit as his platform, he led the black citizenry in nonviolent resistance, a tactic he had learned from studying Mahatma Gandhi, the famed Indian leader. King led thousands of blacks in boycotts, sit-ins, marches and freedom rides and spearheaded political lobbying efforts. To most blacks, he became a hero.

What was King's hero's reward? His house was bombed. He was jailed many times. He endured unjust physical beatings, some by white citizens, some by the police. He was rejected and ridiculed by many white clergyman. His children were ostracized in the schools. The family's belongings were stolen, defaced and burned. Ultimately, of course, this hero was killed for his cause. His ministry was, in many ways, a parallel to that of the apostle Paul.

King was a powerful orator and he was not afraid to use the pulpit for inciting his audience to action. He used the pulpit for more than recruiting, though. His sermons were designed to restore the sense of dignity, self-respect and hope that blacks had lost long ago.

King's message was unusual, challenging blacks to confront the white majority for its mistreatment of blacks. For ages, black Americans had accepted their unfortunate and unjust circumstances as the bad luck of the draw, as a simple and irreversible reality or as the outgrowth of the inherent inadequacies of the black people.

King bristled about such self-doubt. He chided his people for their timidity and self-effacement. He breathed the life of self-value into their hearts and inspired people to put it all on the line for a life that was worth living—one characterized by self-love, dignity and equal justice.

People who grow up in the United States today may have trouble believing how different things were a quarter century ago. King's relentless, mammoth efforts started the revolution and ensured hard-won victories. His perpetual pursuit of a color-blind justice system was instrumental in the Civil Rights Act of 1964 and the Voting Rights Act of 1965. King, the youngest person to win the Nobel Peace Prize, was helping prepare a massive march on the nation's capital in 1968 to raise awareness of the extent and ravages of poverty when he was murdered.

We live in a nation that is still riddled with the cancer of racism, but the enduring legacy of King is that he helped strip segregation and racial prejudice of its moral legitimacy. We acknowledge the presence and the sin of racism today because King would not let us overlook that impropriety.[9]

Ralph Nader

Another Ivy Leaguer joins the list of dominant influence agents of our recent past. Ralph Nader graduated from Princeton University prior to attending Harvard Law School. Always a nonconformist, Nader was disinterested in pursuing a cushy career in corporate law. His passion was to save lives through ensuring social justice. He has

RALPH NADER, AMERICA'S BEST-KNOWN CONSUMER ADVOCATE, HAS BEEN CHIPPING AWAY AT INDUSTRY AFTER INDUSTRY FOR MORE THAN 30 YEARS.

described his life mission as igniting "nothing less than the qualitative reform of the Industrial Revolution."

America's best-known consumer advocate, he has been chipping away at industry after industry for more than 30 years. He may be best known for his battles with the automotive industry. After evaluating the data related to auto accidents, he studied the design of vehicles and emerged with a list of design changes to enhance auto safety. When the auto manufacturers turned a deaf ear to his pleas, he published a book titled *Unsafe At Any Speed*, which catapulted him into the driver's seat in the debate.

Congress passed the 1966 National Traffic and Motor Vehicle Safety Act, largely in response to Nader's constant lobbying. Among the changes it wrought were the padded dashboard, seat headrests, padded steering wheels, a rounded stick shift, nonbreakable glass in the rearview mirror, seat belts and steel-reinforced frames. He advocated air bags 30 years before the auto industry consented to use them. In the first 20 years after passage of the act, more than 100 million cars were recalled for safety violations and design defects.

Nader and his legions of consumer protectors also were key players in current regulations governing meat inspection, imposing limits on radiation exposure, provisions for safe drinking water, lead paint removal, the Environmental Protection Act, asbestos removal and natural gas regulation.

His crowning achievement, though, was the creation and passage of the Freedom of Information Act. That legislation enabled every citizen to gain legal access to public documents. The existence of that law enabled Nader to pioneer citizen-action lawsuits, a means of bringing corporations and governmental agencies into compliance with statutes through simple exercises in litigation.

Nader, like many visionaries, lives a life that is fully consistent with his convictions. He wears clothes he bought at the military PX three decades ago. He does not own or drive a car. He watches his diet carefully and lives in a studio apartment in Washington, D.C. He refuses to drink Coca-Cola (he says every can contains nine teaspoons of sugar) and is an advocate of exercise. His life has been an extension of his vision for a better America.

Your car is safer because of Nader. The quality of the water you drink and the air you breathe may not be perfect, but it is much better than it might have been without Nader's influence.

The corporations of America, as well as the governmental officials we elect, are more responsive to the citizenry and to the legal code because of the Freedom of Information Act. Without Nader casting and pursuing his vision for a new America, government regulations and corporate decision making would be substantially different today.[10]

And There's More

These are just a few of the visionaries who have influenced and changed American life. You and I, whether we like it or not, have reaped the fruit of their vision.

We are also living with the consequences of the vision cast by President Lyndon Johnson, whose Great Society social reforms still constitute a substructure of our welfare system and other government-based services.

We are experiencing the effects of sound-bite journalism, ushered in by journalistic visionaries such as Al Neuharth, whose *USA Today* revolutionized newspaper design and played to the interests of a quick-read audience. Steven Jobs, cofounder of Apple Computers, was largely responsible for taking the machines he helped his friend Steve Wozniak build in the garage and establishing the user-friendly personal computer, which has altered information systems and computing forever.

Robert Moses, the master city planner, deserves the credit—or the blame—for many of the urban-development concepts on which our cities are based. Betty Friedan was the primary mover behind the women's liberation movement of the late 1960s and early '70s. The list of visionaries who have shaped your daily environment and opportunities is long.

<u>32</u>

Visionaries of the 1990s

Can you identify the visionaries of the moment? Sometimes it is hard to tell who is casting vision and who is simply building his or her own empire. A few obvious choices of visionaries, however, are setting the foundation for our lives in the early part of the twenty-first century.

Bill Gates, the power behind Microsoft, is taking computer software to new, life-changing places. John Malone is the dominant player in developing the communications industry, particularly television.

Michael Eisner, CEO of the Walt Disney Company—owners of a multimedia empire that includes ABC—must be regarded as a premier forward thinker as he moves Disney beyond entertainment into new approaches to urban redevelopment.

Can you see the effect of vision upon your life? Think of what your life would be like today if Nader had not remained true to his vision.

What kind of society would we have today if Dewey's theories had never been introduced to teachers and implemented among boomers during their formative years? If Martin Luther King Jr. had not sacrificed his ambitions and talents—and in the end, his life—for the cause of racial equality and human justice, would we be aware of the race relations crisis we have today?

Would you be as concerned about children's exposure to sex on

TV or in the movies, or about the frailty of marriages, or the public acceptance of homosexuality as a moral alternative to heterosexual relationships if Alfred Kinsey had turned his back on his vision for a sexually liberated America?

I cannot imagine anyone intelligently arguing that his or her existence has not been turned upside down by the influence of the visions cast and aggressively pursued by such zealots.

Acknowledging the influence of others upon your life is far removed from your determination to identify God's vision for your life and to invest your entire existence in that perspective.

As a servant of the Father of vision, what will you do to understand God's vision for your life and to invest yourself in the minirevolution He is calling you to shepherd?

Notes

1. Stanley Elkin, "Alfred Kinsey: The Patron Saint of Sex," *Fifty Who Made the Difference* (New York: Esquire Press, Villard Books, 1984), p. 14.
2. Ibid, pp. 13-22; and Judith Reisman and Edward Eichel, *Kinsey, Sex and Fraud* (Lafayette, La.: Huntington House, 1990).
3. Benjamin Spock, *The Common Sense Book of Baby and Child Care* (New York: Dutton, 1946); Harry Stein, "Benjamin Spock's Baby Bible," *Fifty Who Made the Difference* (New York: Esquire Press, Villard Books, 1984), pp. 447-456.
4. John Dewey, *Experience and Education* (New York: Macmillan, 1938).
5. Ibid.
6. Ron Rosenbaum, "The House That Levitt Built," *Fifty Who Made the Difference* (New York: Esquire Press, Villard Books, 1984), pp. 304-320.
7. Ray Kroc, *Grinding It Out* (Chicago: Regnery Company, 1977); Tom Robbins, "Ray Kroc Did It All for You," *Fifty Who Made the Difference* (New York: Esquire Press, Villard Books, 1984), pp. 265-269.
8. Frances Fitzgerald, "The Case of Earl Warren v. Earl Warren," *Fifty Who Made the Difference* (New York: Esquire Press, Villard Books, 1984), pp. 362-369.
9. David Halberstam, "Martin Luther King, American Preacher," *Fifty Who Made the Difference* (New York: Esquire Press, Villard Books, 1984), pp. 237-244.
10. Ken Auletta, "Ralph Nader, Public Eye," *Fifty Who Made the Difference* (New York: Esquire Press, Villard Books, 1984), pp. 407-417.

2

The Nuts and Bolts of Vision

"THERE IS NO MORE POWERFUL ENGINE
DRIVING AN ORGANIZATION TOWARD EXCEL-
LENCE AND LONG-RANGE SUCCESS THAN AN
ATTRACTIVE, WORTHWHILE AND ACHIEVABLE
VISION OF THE FUTURE, WIDELY SHARED."
—BURT NANUS

It is one thing to read the accounts of vision in action or to see the effect of vision implemented. It is another thing altogether to be able to put your finger on exactly what the core concept is—that is, to define vision so succinctly that you can spot the real thing—or a fake—a mile away.

Let's deal with the basics of vision.

Defining Vision

Vision is a clear and precise mental portrait of a preferable future, imparted by God to His chosen servants, based on an accurate under-standing of God, self and circumstances.

Consider the components of God's vision.

Vision is *tangible* to the beholder. Although it is just a concept or perspective of a nonexistent reality, vision exists within the mind of a visionary so clearly that it may be thought of as a living image. Such a vision motivates and directs ministry, filters information, serves as a catalyst in decision making and measures progress.

Changes Will Occur

Vision involves *change*. It enables you to improve a situation. It focus-es on the future and represents a perspective that anticipates the chal-lenges and opportunities to come. *The visionary Christian is one who appreciates the past, lives in the present, but thinks in the future.* That future, if it is to bring pleasure to God, will be significantly different from the reality you experience today.

Vision is *initiated by God, is desired by His people and is conveyed through the Holy Spirit.* God communicates His vision only to those who have persisted in knowing Him intimately, for His vision is a sacred part of unfolding His eternal plan. This means that your motives for seeking a vision are crucial.

Recall the sin of Simon the Sorcerer, who offered Peter money in return for the power of the Holy Spirit and was immediately casti-gated by the apostle for his inappropriate desire (see Acts 8:9-24). He also was disqualified from having the power he craved. Your motives must be pure and your heart willing not only to receive the vision, but also to commit yourself to seeing it come to pass.

Vision is not for the fainthearted. It insinuates a burning desire to devote your life to blessing God through your relentless pursuit of its completion.

A Commitment to Service

Those who commit themselves to His *service* are worthy to receive the vision. That worthiness is demonstrated by the person's passion for God, devotion to Christian service, immersion in God's admonitions and principles and the willingness to fully submit to God's leadership and purposes.

The visionary is one who knows him- or herself well enough to recognize personal faults and limitations, and to therefore rely upon the guidance and the supernatural strength provided by God in the ardent pursuit of the vision.

One of the most impressive qualities of a Christian visionary is his or her *total abandonment of self in favor of complete subjugation to the purposes of God.* This goes far beyond the commitment to Christ for salvation and reflects the absolute surrender to the will of God. Only then is the person truly usable by Him.

The visionary is well aware of the *context* in which the vision must be accomplished, recognizing the seen and unseen obstacles for what they are, and strategically using the human, spiritual and material resources in all vision fulfillment efforts.

God never sets up His trusted servants for failure, but neither does He remove all obstacles and hardships from our paths (see Josh. 1:8,9). He is faithful to those who are diligent in completing the good works He has designed for us.

Vision Will Arrive in His Time

Vision comes when God determines you are *ready to handle it.* When the time is right, God will unveil the vision and will enable you to comprehend the vision. Your ability to grasp that vision is not a matter of human competence, but of spiritual preparation and a wholehearted yearning to obey the vision, no matter what the cost.

Only God knows when we are truly ready for the vision, for it will radically reshape every aspect of our lives, and it will have a special purpose.

37

It is hard for most of us to accept the fact that we have to let God control the schedule for when the vision is conveyed. The rite of passage, though, is worth all the preparation and all the waiting that is required.

If it is not the appropriate time, if you have not sufficiently devoted yourself to His service or if you have not yet completed the growth God desires of you, be assured that you will not be granted the vision.

Clearing Up the Confusion

Vision does not happen in a vacuum. Like all scriptural truths and principles, it is revealed and is made practical in context.

The context of your vision comes from your life mission, values, ministry strategies and tactics, the ministry goals you set, your spiritual gifts, your natural talents and your life experiences.

Mission, vision and *values* represent the **perspectives** you have in relation to ministry. Your *goals, strategies and tactics* flow from those perspectives and result in your ministry **plans.** The remaining elements—your spiritual *gifts,* natural *talents* and life *experiences*—represent the **preparation** provided by God for your ministry.

Let's take a look at these contextual elements.

Perspective

1. Mission

Of the various components we are examining, mission is probably the easiest element to explain and to articulate. The mission of every Christian individual and every Christian church is spelled out for us in the Bible. In brief, mission is the grand purpose for which you or your ministry exists.

Understanding mission facilitates a clear identity, which must precede impact and significance. Mission represents the context within which an individual or organization operates; it is the "big picture," the broadest understanding of the universe within which the individual or corporate actions have meaning and purpose.

You live in a world of opportunities—alternatives too numerous for

> IF YOU ARE SEEKING TO KNOW THE MISSION OF YOUR CHURCH, IT IS TO ENABLE AS MANY PEOPLE AS POSSIBLE TO KNOW, LOVE AND SERVE GOD WITH ALL THEIR HEARTS, SOULS, MINDS AND STRENGTH.

you to fully exploit, too diverse for you to efficiently and effectively address. Unless you embrace some degree of self-definition, you will self-destruct. Think of your mission as the territory within which you will operate. True mission reflects your values, priorities and vision.[1]

For Christians and Christian ministries, the beauty of mission is that God has already defined it. As a disciple of Christ, your life mission is to know, love and serve God with all your heart, soul, mind and strength (see Deut. 6:5; Matt. 22:37-39). Every one of us may pursue this mission in a different manner, but we all live for the same underlying purpose: to please, glorify and honor God.

If you are seeking to know the mission of your church, it is to enable as many people as possible to know, love and serve God with all their hearts, souls, minds and strength. Of course, you can phrase it differently, using terms or language that are more comfortable for you.

Mission can't be mastered. Churches often describe their mission as embracing the five Es: evangelism, exaltation, equipping, extension and encouraging. The essence will be the same, though. We exist to serve God with everything we have. That is the big picture.

You may as well reconcile yourself to the fact that as long as you live and as hard as you try, you will never completely fulfill your mission. Think about it. It is impossible to completely master knowing, loving and serving God with every resource at your disposal. After all, we are human. As fallen creatures, we do not have the capacity to serve Him with perfection. It is a laudable purpose for which to live, however, one that gives us a clear direction to pursue with our lives.

One of the beauties of Christian mission is that it breeds a sense of unity with others. Because we all have the same basic mission, we discover that we have many companions. A true understanding of mission is something that should comfort us through recognizing community and should encourage us through realizing our unity in God's plan.

2. Vision

In comparison to mission, vision is much more focused and detailed. Notice how much leeway your mission provides. In contrast, God's vision will be specific for you and will be unique to you. Vision focuses on what you want the future to be like and your role in creating that particular future.

Nobody else will be granted the same vision as God imparts to you. Why? Because no one else on the planet is exactly like you in terms of gifts, abilities, experiences, opportunities, desires, human attributes and so on. God will customize the vision to fit who you are (see Ps. 138:8).

You can count on being placed in the midst of circumstances where your vision, if faithfully implemented, will be life changing for you and for those touched by the outgrowth of your vision. The vision will be strategic, inspiring, exciting and challenging.

Be a person of influence. Be prepared: accepting God's vision for your life will transform you from a wanderer to a person of influence. It is your way of not only making the most of your life, but also of declaring war against Satan (see Eph. 6:12). Partially because vision means you have chosen your side in the eternal battle and partially because of the realities of seeking to implement significant change in a change-resistant world, turning vision into meaningful action is a bear. Seeing your vision come to life is *never* simple or easy.

Even in the difficulties and hardships that occur during your pursuit of the vision, you will experience great benefits—not the least of which will be a closer partnership with and a deeper reliance upon God.

It is not uncommon for the first reaction to the vision to be, "Naw, that can't be what He intends for me. It's so, so big!" (Compare with Exod. 3:11.) But it may well be exactly what He intends for you. His vision will stretch you in every dimension: intellectually, spiritually and emotionally. Although the vision might seem overwhelming, remember: He never sets us up for failure, only for service and impact, for His purposes.[2]

Gather data, analyze. The vision is discerned through an information gathering and analytical process. This process encompasses praying for guidance and reading the Bible for insights and parameters. It also involves seeking the counsel of others who know us and our context and can be trusted to assist with our best needs in mind, and who will personally and strategically evaluate our context. We also need to interact with colleagues to understand how God is directing them, assess the opportunities and openings and engage in spiritual disciplines, such as fasting.

Discerning the vision is neither straightforward nor predictable. Sometimes it takes a few weeks of diligent effort; sometimes it takes years. The process is perhaps even more important to God than the outcome because the effort we go to draws us closer and closer to Him—which, in itself, is a major value-added condition.[3]

How do you know if what you have arrived at is truly God's vision? We are deluged with impressions, hopes, assumptions and desires. Do those constitute vision? If it is vision, is it human vision or God's vision for a human?

Use the following seven checkpoints to evaluate the veracity of a conclusion you believe may be God's vision.

- *Scriptural.* Test your potential vision against God's Word (see 2 Tim. 3:16,17). He is always perfectly consistent. If anything in the vision conflicts with Scripture, keep searching. You haven't discovered His vision yet. If the notion you are testing is scriptural, continue with the testing. It could be the real thing.
- *Verified.* Meet with those who will be your accountability partners or with those who have been your spiritual mentors and gain their counsel about the likelihood of the conclusion being God's vision for you (see Jer. 4:19; 9:1; 20:9). If these people suggest that you continue to seek the mind of God, take their concerns to heart, perhaps accepting their advice and continuing the search. If, however, they give you the green light, proceed to the next step in the test pattern.
- *Emotion.* It is impossible to receive vision from God and not become excited by it. This is God's special niche for you, His desires for special service in His name. If you are not excited about His vision for your life, you have bigger problems than I can address in this book. Vision generates extreme enthusiasm and a sense of anticipation in the life

of the beholder. If you think you have discovered God's vision and you are not bursting with newfound energy and anticipation, keep searching. If you are champing at the bit, try the next test.

- *Fear.* God's vision is a holy and wonderful thing. The fact that He loves us enough to spare us from the eternal consequences we so richly deserve is mind-boggling enough (see Prov. 1:7; 9:10; Isa. 6:5-8; Jer. 1:5,6). But then to receive a vision for a life-changing, world-transforming ministry is overwhelming. We are totally inadequate to accomplish the vision He has intended for us. If you are not awed by the vision, you don't have it. If you feel incapable of making it real or unworthy of the task He has set before you, that is how His vision usually feels to those who get it. Next test...

THROUGH GOD'S SUPERNATURAL BLESSINGS AND EMPOWERMENT, YOU PROBABLY WILL PRODUCE THINGS YOU NEVER DREAMED OF AND WILL MATURE IN WAYS YOU THOUGHT WERE DESIGNED ONLY FOR THE SPIRITUAL SUPERSTARS.

41

- *Uniqueness.* God's vision is like a fingerprint. No other vision like it exists in the entire world because you are unique in terms of circumstances, resources, abilities and opportunities (see Ps. 139:1-18). If your vision is a ho-hum vision, one that is the same as someone else's, then you have not reached the target. God's vision makes you totally unique in the grand scheme of global ministry, whether you are a world-famous leader or a new Christian barely known to your congregation of 50 people. If your vision is unique, see if it meets the next criterion.
- *Difficulty.* God's vision is beyond what you can do on your own power. If it were any other way, why would He need to implant that vision in you? His vision will stretch you beyond anything you have ever accomplished; maybe beyond anything you have contemplated in the past (see 1 Chron. 28:20; Phil. 4:13). The beauty of pursuing God's vision is that it enables you to maximize your capabilities, pushing you beyond what you thought were your limits. Through God's supernatural blessings and empowerment you probably will produce things you never

dreamed of and will mature in ways you thought were designed only for the spiritual superstars. Vision maximizes your potential.

- *Worthiness.* Vision from God is something that is worthy of your fullest, deepest commitment. Is this vision something you would die for? Is it something for which you would sacrifice those material and intangible things that have been dear to you (see Phil. 1:20-24)? God wants all of you, every thought, every effort, every word, every relationship and every resource. He does not want these things just for the sake of expanding the heavenly stockpile of stuff. He wants them because they reflect our intense commitment to His highest hopes and dreams for our lives. Does the vision demonstrably increase your determination to devote everything you possess to the fulfillment of the vision?

Vision is too critical to ignore, to squander or to misunderstand. It is the heart of the perspective you must bring into your life.

3. Values

Values are the nonnegotiable characteristics you want reflected in your life. When you consider values, you are determining who you want to be—that is, the kind of character you wish to develop (see Phil. 4:8,9).

Values define the person. Amazingly, millions of Americans have never devoted serious thought to identifying what kind of person they want to be. Most people have default values—a series of values that minimize the friction between personal spiritual inclinations, personal emotional preferences, cultural expectations and relational pressures. Default values are flexible values because the person's needs and preferences can change with each shift in the context of life.

The essence of the Bible is about developing character (see Heb. 12:1-11). The lives of the great Bible heroes, as well as the profound teachings throughout the pages of Scripture, tell us much about values. If a person is sincerely committed to Christian maturity, godly values are being pursued. Chapter 6 is entirely devoted to a more extensive discussion of values.

Plans

4. Goals

For all the attention goal setting receives in the media, in business environments and in private conversations, goals remain relatively rare in the lives of churches and Christians.

According to my research, fewer than 1 out of every 10 Christian adults sets specific goals for life in any given year. The proportion is not much better among churches.

Goals are the ends we wish to accomplish within a specified time frame. For an outcome to be a goal, it must be measurable. Thus, goals typically identify what is to be accomplished in some quantifiable form and by what deadline. The goal may allude to budget realities, methods and who is to be involved in reaching the goal.

5. Strategies

It takes a particular approach to reach the desired outcome of the goals you wish to accomplish. The approaches you choose are your strategies. Effective strategies are not formed in a vacuum. They must be related to mission, vision and goals. You may have multiple strategies for each goal you hope to accomplish. On average, three to five are selected.

Strategies are the answer to your question: How can I achieve my goals? As such, strategies are not truly measurable. Their purpose is to give short-term direction.

6. Tactics

Tactics are where the rubber meets the road. A tactic is what you do in a strategic fashion to meet your goal. Tactics are the implementation phase. They come in many shapes and sizes, including programs, rules and policies, events, communications, relationships or any other intentional behavior designed to achieve your goal.

Just as every goal needs multiple strategies to succeed, so each strategy needs multiple tactics. Tactics are the specific, tangible actions in which people engage. They should be consistent with the strategy, developed to reach the goal, demonstrate a person's values, emerge from the vision and be compatible with mission.

Typically, when we evaluate what a person does, we evaluate the nature and fulfillment of that person's tactics. It is not unusual to have a dozen or more tactics related to a single strategy. Each tactic is designed to accomplish one part of the strategy to which it is related. The accomplishment of a single strategy requires the completion of many tactical activities.

A great strategist is one who is able not only to conceive wise and effective strategies, but also one who can then break down the strategy into many components—the individual actions that must take place to fulfill the strategy. A great strategy without well-conceived and fully implemented tactics is incomplete.

The interrelationship of these elements in planning is illustrated by the effect of the absence of an element. A goal without strategy or a strategy without tactics is a concept without a prayer.

Preparation

7. Spiritual Gifts

Spiritual gifts are the invisible, but perceptible, empowerments given by God to believers for special service.

The Bible is clear in stating that every believer has at least one spiritual gift (see 1 Pet. 4:10), and that the purpose of those gifts is to enable the believer to do the will of God for the benefit of others (see Rom. 12:1,2; 1 Cor. 12:7). The Bible lists 27 spiritual gifts, most of which can be found in one of five passages about gifts (see Rom. 12:6-8; 1 Cor. 12:8-10, 28-30; Eph. 4:11; 1 Pet. 4:9-11). You have at least one of those gifts as God's way of preparing you to do things that on your own strength, development and ability you cannot accomplish.

Spiritual gifts also are meant to form a complementary matrix within the Body of Christ, to be used in a seamless web of interlocking efforts that build the Church. As you strive to fulfill your vision, you will have the exact gift or gifts necessary to pull your weight in the accomplishment of your spiritual task.[4]

Spiritual Gifts Identified in the Bible

Administration	Knowledge
Apostle	Leadership
Celibacy	Martyrdom
Deliverance	Mercy
Discerning of Spirits	Miracles
Evangelism	Missionary
Exhortation	Pastor
Faith	Poverty (Voluntary)
Giving	Prophecy
Healing	Service
Helps	Teaching
Hospitality	Tongues
Intercession	Wisdom
Interpretation	

8. Talents

God has also invested in you some abilities we call "talents." Some people have a talent for building relationships, some can speak persuasively, others can perform complex mathematical functions. The breadth of talents found in humanity appear to be endless.

Like spiritual gifts, however, natural talents do not arise randomly. God designed you in an intentional manner, gave you every ability and resource you need to accomplish His objectives. The talents you have may be "natural" (i.e., available to you without much nurturing or honing) or they may be learned and hard earned. You have some talents, though, that are perfect for God's vision for you.

Those talents are just one more way God has prepared you for the

> YOUR EXPERIENCES PROVIDE YOU WITH INSIGHTS, SKILLS AND RESOURCES THAT WILL BE CRUCIAL TO YOUR COMMITMENT TO, AND IMPLEMENTATION OF, THE VISION.

fulfillment of the vision. Recognizing your talents can help you gain a better understanding of your vision and will prove invaluable in your ongoing effort to complete your personal vision and to play your role in the pursuit of your church's vision.

45

9. Experiences

During the course of your life, you have had ample opportunity to test, to refine and to enjoy your spiritual gifts and your natural talents. The cumulative effect of your experiences has been to prepare you to "do the vision."

It is like the practice, study and prayer involved in preparing for an athletic event such as the Super Bowl or a World Series game. Every game you have played has been one more step in preparing to be a champion.

Your experiences are a vital part of your preparation for what God has enlisted you to do. They will provide you with insights, skills and resources that will prove to be crucial to your commitment to, and implementation of, the vision.

Product

Effective Ministry

At some point in your life, you will be ready to discern God's vision and then to make it the centerpiece of your existence. Maximizing who you are for God's purposes will result in each of the nine elements just described working in harmony to move you along the path to ultimate service.

For instance, to identify and understand your mission, vision and values will require you to apply some natural talents and abilities and may draw on your life experiences. Reaching your goals will be a matter of using your gifts and talents, but not until you have developed strategies and tactics based on your comprehension of the mission, vision and values.

Once you are aware of these elements and how they work in tandem, your life will be a more fascinating study in the complexities God orchestrates in each one of us to effectively serve His purposes.

Contextual Elements of Vision

Perspective:	mission, vision, values
Plans:	goals, strategies, tactics
Preparation:	gifts, talents, experiences
Product:	effective ministry

Beware of the Traps

As you might expect, you will encounter a few traps.

One of them is a terminology trap. Is mission the big picture or is vision the big picture? Is vision the same as calling? What is a purpose, as opposed to mission or vision? Are goals the same as objectives?

I firmly believe that using vocabulary as a snare is one of Satan's clever strategies for throwing you off track before you can make a big impact for Christ. To be honest, the words you use to describe any of the concepts we are addressing does not matter; what does matter is your heart, your commitment and your clarity in understanding and action. Words are merely contrived symbols that have a common meaning and therefore permit communication, discovery and progress. Thus, any words are appropriate that will allow you to know, love and serve God with all your heart, mind and soul in harmony with the special purposes for which He has created you.

A more direct answer to each of these queries is also in order. The dominant usage of mission and vision in the business world is the same as that used in this book—namely, mission is the biggest view of your possible reason for existence, and vision is the narrower definition of your unique approach to creating a preferable future.

Vision and calling are related, but are different. A calling is something that is vocational in nature, something that provides a broad sense of direction for life within the general framework of our mission.

Vision is what you will seek to achieve within the parameters of your calling. For instance, we speak of a person having a calling to full-time pastoral ministry. That is more specific than mission, but not specific enough to be thought of as vision. The person who is called to ministry may have a vision of serving as a pastor to AIDS patients and develop a caring community among those people. The person will administer the love and care the patients need and deserve, and intentionally strive to restore their sense of belonging, dignity and family relationships.

"Purpose" is a term used by several large denominations—most notably the Southern Baptists—which is synonymous with mission.

Goals are spoken of differently in different contexts. Sometimes you will hear goals referred to as the desired outcomes, and objectives are the outcomes made measurable. For instance, a goal might be to help people overcome their drug addictions. The objective might be to help 100 people end their addictions to cocaine during the next 12 months.

47

Don't become diverted by senseless arguments about language. Focus on what is important: getting a sense of God's perspective for your life (i.e., mission, vision and values), having a plan of action (i.e., goals, strategies and tactics) and maximizing the ways God has prepared you for effective Christian service (i.e., knowing and exploiting your spiritual gifts, natural talents and past experiences).

Matching Visions

So let's say you have come all this way and you are able to identify your vision from God and are excited about devoting the rest of your life to making it real. What happens when you attend your church next week and discover that its vision is different from yours?

Don't panic. Chapter 9 addresses that question. Briefly, you should examine your vision and that of your church and determine if any aspects of your respective visions overlap. If so, focus on how to create harmony by allowing the area of overlap (i.e., the points of intersection) to become the glue that holds the two together. If no such points exist, you then have two options.

First, speak with the leaders of the church and jointly seek God's guidance in finding some previously unidentified points of intersection. If that effort does not result in a satisfacory outcome, you may simply seek a different church home, one that has a vision for ministry that clearly coincides with your personal heartbeat as reflected in your vision.

What if you are ministering within a church that has articulated a vision from God? Should the ministry in which you are involved, one of the programs or departments, have a separate vision statement? Ideally, yes, as long as that vision statement is clearly subordinate to that of the church at large and is clearly complementary to the vision of the church. Why have a separate vision statement for a class, a program, a department or a ministry? Because it helps to clarify and focus. It fuels the passion. It provides a special identity within the true Body. If handled properly, this can serve to enhance the effect and the focus of the ministry. Unless internal power games are being played, this should not create problems.

Notes

1. For a more extensive discussion of the differences between vision and mission, see George Barna, *The Power of Vision* (Ventura, Calif.: Regal Books, 1992), chapters 2 and 3.
2. In *The Power of Vision*, I discussed the definition of vision and its core components, the relationship of vision to leadership, the distinction between mission and vision, misperceptions and myths that hinder a person or group from experiencing true vision, the difference between human vision and vision from God, the process of discerning God's vision, the characteristics of God's vision, the benefits of, and obstacles to grasping vision, and the key means of articulating the vision.
3. A more detailed discussion of this process of ascertaining the vision is included in Chapter 6 of *The Power of Vision*.
4. Spiritual gifts are a fascinating, if controversial, part of the process. For a good primer about spiritual gifts, including a "gift test" to help you determine what gift or gifts God may have given you, consult C. Peter Wagner's *Your Spiritual Gifts Can Help Your Church Grow* (Ventura, Calif.: Regal Books, 1979; revised edition, 1994).

CHAPTER

3

Radical Christians

> "GIVE ME A MAN WHO SAYS 'THIS ONE
> THING I DO' AND NOT 'THESE FIFTY
> THINGS I DABBLE IN.'"
> —D. L. MOODY

The essence of vision for you, as a Christian, is radical obedience to God's special calling upon your life. Vision is not always the easiest route to follow. The pursuit of God's vision is usually not about taking the most enjoyable or personally desirable avenue toward a given outcome. Sometimes, following God's vision for your life is not even the most logical path to pursue. In all cases, however, a total commitment to God's vision for your life is the most appropriate and the most honorable course of action.

The Bible provides for us many examples of how God intervenes in the lives of His most devoted followers and directs them in unexpected ways. Often, believers who seek and implement His vision find it is at odds with the initial desires of their hearts, which requires them to reorient their priorities.

Christians who dedicate themselves to implementing God's vision for their lives commonly discover that their choices demand they avoid some attractive opportunities available to them in the world. Frequently, Christian visionaries who pursue God's special plan live in defiance against the odds. In most cases, we find that the followers of Christ who commit to God's vision endure ridicule and abuse as direct results of their commitments.

From a worldly perspective, following God's vision for your life may not be the most appealing lifestyle. Those who dedicate themselves to making God's vision real do so for one reason: to do anything less would cheat God and His creation. Anything less than complete obedience to His peculiar path for them would be to settle for a life that is less meaningful, less fulfilling and less responsive to God.

Biblical Examples

We encounter example after example of people in the Bible who matured in their faith to the point where they were ready to totally sell out to God. At some point in our lives, we realize that the Christian faith is about much more than mere salvation.

I don't mean to minimize the significance of eternal spiritual security. Salvation is God's gift to us through the substitutionary death of His Son, Jesus Christ. Christianity is not based on us earning God's favor, for our very nature (i.e., sinful) precludes that possibility. The holiest person in the world is still a failure in God's eyes unless that person has submitted his or her life to Jesus Christ and has acknowledged that apart from Christ eternal hope is not possible.

Those of us who have submitted our lives to Christ and truly allow Him to direct them and to use them as He sees fit have acknowledged that accepting the gift is just one step toward our maturation as devotees of Christ.

A true disciple of Jesus is not content to simply revel in eternal security. The authentic follower of Christ is committed to growing in an honest and profound relationship with God. One important outgrowth of that pursuit is our desire to be a more serious and reliable servant of the King, not as a way to gain stature or heavenly brownie points, but as a reflection of our deep love for God Himself.

It is not enough to simply take the gift and to revel in it; a mark of maturity is that we hunger to invest our time on earth in activities that have spiritual significance. Such meaning comes by understanding how He created us and how we can employ every resource at our disposal—time, energy, money, relationships, materials, knowledge—to unfold God's ultimate plan for humankind. This requires discovering and pursuing His vision for us.

Ever the thoughtful and faultless teacher, God provided examples of fellow visionaries for our examination. In the Old Testament, I count at least two dozen visionaries we might study. Those stalwarts of God's purposes include Abraham, Josiah, Joseph, Judah, Moses, Joshua, Deborah, Gideon, David, Solomon, Hezekiah and Nehemiah.

The New Testament is equally generous, providing a cast of visionaries that stretches from John the Baptist to the apostle Paul, encompassing at least another 20 stalwarts of the faith.

The Bible does not use the term "vision" as it is used today.[1] That does not mean, however, that the Bible is silent about the importance and necessity of vision. The Bible never uses the terms "abortion," "racial prejudice" or "white-collar crime" either, but no intelligent Christian would argue that God's Word offers no counsel on those issues. We can learn fundamental truths about vision by evaluating the perspectives and experiences of the visionaries God shaped, elevated and deployed for His purposes as recorded in Scripture.

In the first chapter, we considered the effect of visionaries whose visions were designed to satisfy their personal desires or whims. To those people, significance was determined by their own values, by the accolades they received from the world and by their personal goals for life. But the Bible clearly teaches a crucial alternative approach to, and application of, vision.

Let's look at a few people who devoted their lives to convert God's vision into action, for the glory of God and, consequently, for the benefit of humankind.

51

Abraham

Abraham was in the driver's seat of life before God got his attention. Well educated and affluent, Abraham was hardly a down-and-out loser who needed God's special blessings to enjoy meaning or purpose in life. He chose to follow God, however, and to dedicate his life to obedience to God. As a result, he spent the final 100 years of his life seeking God's direction to make the vision a reality.

The Response Was Immediate

We know little about the first 75 years of Abraham's life. We do know, however, that his relationship with God was deep enough that when God communicated to him a vision for the future, Abraham did more than just listen. He immediately and completely redefined his life to be fully obedient to God's vision for his remaining years (see Gen. 12:1-3).

Being obedient was no small undertaking. It meant leaving his relatives, his friends, his countrymen and women, his land and everything that was secure and comfortable. Abraham's experience demonstrated that following God's vision always carries with it a substantial earthly price. Besides a total change in lifestyle, his story is one of broken relationships, physical hardships, emotional highs and lows and occasional doubts and misunderstandings in his relationship with God.

The Path Is Not Painless

A life based on vision focuses on delivering a superior future, but it does not necessarily mean the path to that future is direct, rapid and painless. Often we assume that God wants us to be successful on our terms. In reality, the example of the visionaries in the Bible shows that He wants us to be successful on His terms. Success, in His eyes, means absolute obedience to His vision and His ways.

For Abraham, pursuing God's vision entailed family disputes and deaths, suffering God's perfect but painful justice, participating in bloody military skirmishes, instituting a painful ritual to show spiritual solidarity with God (i.e., circumcision), addressing sexual perversions enjoyed by the people and confronting people guilty of other transgressions and shortsightedness (see Gen. 13:1-7; 14:1-24; 16:1-16; 17:1-17; 18:1-33).

Abraham, however, remained focused on the vision (i.e., claiming a new land for a new people who would become the spiritual kinfolk of God Almighty). God blessed his efforts to be obedient.

Abraham Remained Humble

The example left for us by Abraham includes another crucial factor: his continual humility before God. Many times during his interaction with God, he built an altar and worshiped God (see Gen. 12:7—13:18; 22:9). Therein lies a major distinction between those who pursue God's vision and those who live to bring their own vision to fruition.

The Bible does not provide much direct insight into Abraham's spiritual development; however, by studying his behavior, we can know his heart. Why did God choose Abraham? A major reason was that Abraham had made a lifelong practice of obeying and worshiping God—hallmarks of a usable leader—one with whom God's vision would be safe and diligently implemented.

Abraham was outlived by the vision, as are many other visionary leaders. Although he set his eyes on the goal, he brought his people to the brink of the goal, but did not personally experience the total fulfillment of God's vision. Even so, Abraham would not have been disappointed because the true mark of a visionary is not reaching the destination so much as it is the growth and fulfillment gained on the journey.

An All-Star Team Member

Abraham is a mainstay on the Visionary All-Star team. We know him as "the father of Israel," the first post-flood leader of God's people and as one of the patriarchs of the Judeo-Christian faith. His stature is attested to by his inclusion in the "hall of faith" in Hebrews 11. Without his leadership and his example of unwavering commitment to the vision, human history would have been entirely different.

Moses

Moses is a study in contrasts. He was born to Jewish parents, but was reared by the Egyptian ruler. He was God's chosen man for the times, yet he had murdered a countryman just prior to being selected by God. He was a well-educated man leading a band of shepherds and

> MOSES CAUGHT THE VISION, ARTICULATED THE VISION AND IMPLEMENTED THE VISION BASED ON HIS FAITH AND WHOLEHEARTED TRUST IN AN OMNIPOTENT AND LOVING GOD.

unschooled people. He lacked confidence in his public speaking abilities, yet we know him for his public pronouncements to the people of Israel and their enemies. Moses' ministry might be viewed as an effort to strike a balance between tough love for the people and compassion toward them (see Exod. 2:1-10,12; 4:10).

Moses' significance cannot be slighted. He was indisputably God's chosen man for the times, selected to lead the people into the Promised Land. The journey was a time for refining people's hearts, as Moses constantly sought to clarify God's holiness, His expectations and His faithfulness to a disloyal, doubting, sinful and complaining people.

Envisioning a New Land
Why did Moses, the adopted son of a Pharaoh, highly educated and wealthy, leave his life of comfort and pleasure in favor of leading his people through decades of hardship? Because God gave him a vision of a new life in a land of milk and honey in which they would be free from oppression and connected to the greatest power in the universe. Moses caught the vision, articulated the vision and implemented the vision based on his faith and wholehearted trust in an omnipotent and loving God.

Moses' story is a fascinating profile in visionary leadership. Consider the obstacles. He asked God to grant him a companion who could compensate for his self-perceived weakness in public speaking and was given Aaron. Much to Moses' eventual chagrin, Aaron proved to be a spiritual anchor more than a spiritual leader, regularly compromising God's truth and principles to gain people's favor. The partner Moses needed as a source of strength ultimately became a source of frustration (see 4:10-16; 32:1-4).

The Obstacles Multiplied

Aaron was not the only obstacle in Moses' path. Despite being called by God for His special blessing, the Israelites were not strong in their faith, complained continually, doubted and resisted God (and Moses). Moses' adopted father, the Pharaoh of Egypt, rejected Moses' request for the freedom to leave, necessitating Moses to issue the 10 plagues God instructed him to send against the Egyptian ruler and his people (see Exod. 5:21; 7:1—11:10; Num. 14:1,2).

Later, Moses had to lead the people in flight while being pursued by the Egyptian army. The people of God then lived in a desert for decades, existed on something less than gourmet food and had no real sense of direction, timing or coming victory. Moses himself was banned from entry into the land of promise because of his disobedience to God (see Exod. 14:1—25:21; Num. 13:17—36:13; Deut. 34:4).

Amazingly, though, Moses remained the leader of the people and brought them closer to the ultimate destination. He was driven by his vision to serve God rather than to cave in to the will of the people or to pursue his personal desires.

Moses' personal will vanished, as did that of every visionary leader we see in Scripture, and his newly established passion for the future was indistinguishable from God's will for Moses' life. All it took was for Moses to surrender his personal goals, desires and dreams in favor of those provided supernaturally by God.

Vision Is Not a Simple Process

I love Moses' story because it shows us that vision is not always a simple process of hearing from the Lord and accepting and following the vision. In Exodus 3 and 4, we read how Moses debated the vision with God. The partnership with Aaron shows us that a visionary cannot be effective simply by communicating vision, as Aaron was supposed to do, but also must live in harmony with the vision.

Moses' path toward the land of promise was filled with revelation as God shared bits and pieces of the goals, strategies and tactics to facilitate the realization of the vision. Those progressive insights were accessible to Moses only because of his constant and intense communication with God, his peerless leader.

Joshua

Joshua provides an entirely different perspective about visionary leadership. God gave Moses the vision. Joshua inherited the vision, in a refined state, and was called to complete the work of his predecessor and mentor, Moses (see Josh. 1:1-4).

Because Moses had sinned (see Num. 20:10) and was disqualified from entering the new place of hope and freedom, the mantle of leadership was passed to Joshua. This strikes me as analogous to passing the torch of leadership from one pastor to another within many of our churches. In that case, the vision from God is intended for the congregation—not the pastor—and the departure of one senior leader does not negate the vision, but simply transfers its leadership to another trusted person within His kingdom.

Vision Can Be Refined

Joshua's experience also demonstrates that the vision can be refined in a certain time period. When Moses began to lead the Israelites out of Egypt and into the wilderness, their primary vision was to leave one place for another and to experience God's glory and blessings in the process.

During Joshua's era, the vision added another dimension: cleansing the land through military conquest and settlement. Often the core of the vision remains unchanged, but the fine points of its implementation may well change in response to how God's people have responded to Him and His vision during the course of time. Indeed, the tenor of the vision during Joshua's leadership shifted from achieving freedom from oppression (see Exod. 3:7-10) to achieving rest in a new location (see Ps. 95:11).

As does every visionary leader, Joshua had to address major barriers to successfully implement the vision. First, he inherited not only a vision, but also a polytheistic group of followers. Second, he was the leader casting vision to a group of inveterate sinners. It wasn't enough that God had given evidence of Himself time after time after time through the directives to Moses and then to Joshua. Third, the deceitful behavior of Achan caused Israel to suffer an unexpected and unnecessary military setback on its way to ultimate victory (see Josh. 7:1-26).

The Goal: To Exemplify Holiness

In all instances, Joshua's determination to exemplify holiness enabled him to help the nation surpass its weaknesses and to be restored in God's eyes. Joshua was not going to let the vision die simply because of the ignorance, stubbornness and hard-heartedness of the people. He was on the trail of something bigger and better than any of these people could ever have imagined. Joshua was possessed by the vision of God, and nothing was going to deter him from its realization.

The beauty of Joshua's story is that it shows the character required to become a true visionary. Joshua exemplified courage in the face of danger. He demonstrated the virtues of strategic thinking and service. Most of all, he reflected the influence of absolute obedience.

The Bible tells us what a tremendous military strategist and warrior Joshua was, but it also confirms that without the power and blessing of God, Joshua would have been little more than a footnote in ancient history. The difference between having been an accomplished soldier and a great leader who left an everlasting legacy was the understanding, casting and dogged pursuit of God's vision.

Josiah

Israel had many kings. Josiah was one of its greatest, if among its least renowned. Although he assumed the throne at the age of eight and followed the horrific half-century rule of his father, Manasseh, Josiah was perhaps the most moral king in Israel's checkered history (see 2 Kings 22:1—23:30).

By the time he was in his mid-teens, the "boy-king" had discerned God's vision for his kingship: to restore the God of Israel to the throne of the culture through pure worship, the destruction of all vestiges of idolatry, the restoration of the Temple and a zealous emphasis upon just and righteous living.

To comprehend how breathtaking a vision this was, we need to recall the extensive moral and spiritual corruption that prevailed during the reign of Manasseh (see 2 Kings 21:1-18). It required astounding courage and determination not only to renounce the defining practices of Josiah's father, but also to confront the power brokers, the vested interests and the comfortable corruptions of the day. No 16-year-old I have ever known has had such fortitude.

The sole explanation for this boldness is Josiah's encounter with the living God, resulting in his insatiable desire to know Him and to serve Him as deeply and purely as humanly possible. Josiah understood that Israel was fighting a losing battle in its defiance of God. He devoted his life to achieve peace with God for the nation.

Reforms Instituted

During his reign, Josiah instituted countless religious reforms, restored the justice system and led the people to a new lifestyle that was reflective of the righteousness demanded by God. His legend grew as he destroyed idols and pagan altars, spearheaded redeveloping the Temple and led the people in huge religious celebrations and in a public renewal of the nation's covenant with God.

Josiah was single-handedly responsible for one of the greatest religious reformations in human history. His efforts were so sincere that God refrained from destroying Judah for its evil. One of the great lessons from Josiah's life is that it is never too late to return to God no matter how despicable our lives have been.

The story of Josiah shows us something else about visionaries. Despite Josiah being fully engrossed in service to God and being a leader whose passion was to do justice and righteousness, the people observed and followed his example, but their hearts never changed. Upon his death, just 31 years after taking the throne, the people returned to the dark ways that had made Josiah's kingship so incredible.

The Vision Must Be Shared
Sadly, we learn that a visionary who does not adequately sell the vision to the people does them an injustice. Historical documents explain that the people were smitten by Josiah's zeal and earnestness. He was a charismatic leader, inciting the people to reform on the strength of his commitment to God. The people did not really understand his devotion to the God of their forefathers, but they agreed to his terms of reform because they appreciated his character and intentions. At the time of Josiah's death, they reverted to what comes naturally to humankind—selfish, godless and sinful living—because they had never truly embraced the motivations underlying his vision.

Josiah's pursuit of the vision was not wasted. Many people's lives were permanently changed for the better by Josiah's reforms. Thousands of people, drawing on their own searches for the true God and their personal desires to live righteous lives, were able to extrapolate the reasons behind Josiah's idiosyncrasies. What could have become a revolution of holiness, however, became merely a time-out in a protracted movement of wretchedness because of Josiah's failure to sell the vision.

Nehemiah

Every group has its spiritual center and its symbols of strength and solidarity. For the Jews in the fifth century B.C., the spiritual center was Jerusalem; the symbol of their unity and might was the Temple (see Neh. 1—13).

For seven decades, the Temple had been left in disrepair. The spiritual condition of the Jews was not much better. When this came to the attention of Nehemiah, a Jew serving as a trusted confidant of King Artaxerxes, it pierced his heart. He wept about the deterioration of

God's people and sought direction from the Lord through an extended period of prayer and fasting. He sought a vision from God for how to serve his true King most appropriately. God answered by imparting a vision that would change the lives of millions of people forever.

Vision Led to Recovery
The vision that emerged was for a total recovery of the nation of Israel, initiated by rallying the people of God to rebuild the walls and gates of Jerusalem, thereby facilitating religious reforms and the spiritual revival of the Jews.

NEHEMIAH'S STORY PROVIDES FOR US PERHAPS THE MOST CLEAR-CUT CASE STUDY OF A VISIONARY LEADER IN ACTION.

This may sound simple, but remember that Israel was a scattered people at this point. They lacked a spiritual leader, a spiritual focus and a spiritual purpose. The idea of collecting the necessary resources—talented people, money, building materials, physical security and emotional confidence—would have seemed ludicrous.

That is why we can never hope to institute significant change in the world on the basis of human vision. Our efforts will never be sufficiently supplied or focused to sustain the effort needed to create lasting, meaningful change. Fortunately, God had been preparing Nehemiah for this moment in history, and Nehemiah was willing to risk everything—ranging from his cushy position in the palace to his life—in the pursuit of this daunting, but God-inspired challenge.

Demonstrating extreme faith and laudable people skills, Nehemiah led the rebuilding process. He motivated the people on the basis of the vision, not just by reconstructing a building, but by resurrecting the self-esteem and the spiritual focus of the Jews. He accumulated the wealth of talent and resources needed to accomplish the task, and he did so in spite of the political threat a united Jewish community would have represented.

Nehemiah masterfully navigated through a maze of personal taunts, threats and challenges. He organized and delegated efficiently and effectively. He confronted Israel's skeptics and enemies to create a peaceful environment that allowed the workers to complete the project. Incredibly, the walls were rebuilt in less than two months. Then came the more arduous and more meaningful task of rebuilding the spiritual lives of the Jews.

A Visionary in Action

Nehemiah's story provides for us perhaps the most clear-cut case study of a visionary leader in action. It starts with information about the conditions of the day. Informed about reality, Nehemiah questioned his life focus and was driven to his knees in impassioned prayer.

When God answered his prayers, Nehemiah ran with the vision, devoting his full attention and every resource he could muster to its fulfillment. He overcame the many obstacles that invariably challenge a visionary with responses and skills that come from reliance upon prayer. The vision had power because it was from God, because it was blessed by God and because Nehemiah was completely committed to its implementation. This latter reality was exhibited by the fervor with which he threw himself into the tasks at hand.

One of the outstanding attributes of Nehemiah, like the other biblical visionaries we encounter, is that he was driven to righteousness. Like Abraham, Noah, David, Josiah and Joshua, Nehemiah was an imperfect creature striving to become holy for the glory of his Creator. People were captivated by the vision Nehemiah articulated, partially because he was so certain of its origin and so determined to see it fulfilled. He not only called people to action, but he also led them in appropriate action.

59

Peter

Although Paul receives credit for being the most significant initiator of new churches in Christian history, the truth is that Peter was the initial church planter. God's vision, instilled in his heart, was to create a true community of believers in Jerusalem.

Having been mentored in spiritual development for three years by Jesus, Peter set out to organize a spiritual family that was identifiable by its core attributes: sharing, learning, helping, worshiping, evangelizing, praying and loving. At the end of Acts 2, we discover such a community of Christ devotees. That congregation became the mother church of all the future Christian churches in the world.

Single-Minded and Courageous

Based on his exploits with Jesus, Peter is widely known for his impulsive behavior (see Matt. 16:22). In a discussion of his ability to promote God's vision, however, we cannot afford to overlook some of his more useful qualities, such as his single-mindedness and his courage once the Resurrection had taken place.

The big fisherman put all his natural fears and concerns aside in a laserlike focus on creating an assembly of Christians in Jerusalem that would neither shun its responsibilities to reach out nor would become sidetracked in its opportunities to serve each other's spiritual, material and emotional needs.

The visionary behavior of Peter is inspiring. In some instances, we see the ex-coward risking his life through his complete obedience to his vision (see Acts 5:29).

In other situations, we observe Peter refusing to rest on his laurels as one of the Lord's inner circle, or as a high-profile spokesperson for the nascent Church. Instead, he demonstrated humility, integrity and a desire for deeper spiritual growth (see Acts 10,11).

Peter matured into a person God could trust with a vision that was central to the birthing of the organized community of faith.

Paul

Seeking forgiveness is one thing. Turning from a leading persecutor of a people to one of their primary defenders, apologists and trainers is another. After God had the attention of Saul of Tarsus, such a transformation took place. Paul became one of the most prolific evangelists of all time, thanks to his understanding of God's vision for his life.

Nobody knows how the change in his life transpired in the years immediately after Paul's encounter with Christ on the road to Damascus. Having studied visionaries and their behaviors, though, my hypothesis is that the three years Paul spent in the desert shortly after his conversion was a time when he sought the Lord in earnest, after which he emerged with a vision to reach the unreached outside Judea and Samaria (see Acts 9:1-8; Gal. 1:18).

The First Church Planter

Always zealous for whatever cause he believed in, Paul returned from the desert as intense and driven as ever. What is intriguing is the nature of his thrust from his post-desert experience. It is different from what might have been expected.

Given his background—an upwardly mobile leader among the Jews, highly educated, religious to a fault, familiar with the people and power brokers of Judea and Samaria—we might reasonably expect Paul to have focused his energies on interacting with the people he knew, in the region he knew, within the customs and traditions he knew.

Instead, Paul noted again and again that God called him to evangelize the Gentiles through logical, public presentations of the gospel and to form them into new churches. Those new church bodies were initiated in areas outside his stamping grounds, making him the first international Christian evangelist and church planter (see Rom. 15:7-21).

Paul's Epistles also indicate that he believed God's vision for his life required him to go beyond evangelizing and organizing and to include helping new believers to mature in their faith so that they might reproduce themselves spiritually.

A Startling Journey

None of this sounds radical to us today. I have read through Paul's Epistles a hundred times without recognizing what a startling journey he was on. Sure, we revel at the determination he showed in the face of extreme adversity, but most of us don't give a second thought to the nature of his day-to-day ministry. Why? Because your ministry, mine and that of almost every church in America is based upon Paul's notion of individual and corporate spiritual development. Essentially, we are still mimicking Paul's lead today.

The Vision Lives On

God gave Paul a vision that has outlived the wild man from Tarsus by nearly 2,000 years. The religious life of people during the time of Christ was different from that which emerged in response to Christ's life, death and resurrection. The groundbreaking ministry strategies and tactics employed by Paul did not exist prior to his conversion. Paul was the prototypical churchman.

61

Almost single-handedly, through the vision of God and empowerment of His Holy Spirit, Paul made the Church of Christ an international movement of faith. His actions were unquestionably innovative. The other apostles and church leaders in Jerusalem were somewhat taken aback by his itinerant ministry and his organizing of Gentile believers on foreign shores. Paul was so far ahead of his time that we usually overlook his perch on the leading edge of ministry, but only because time has finally caught up with him and has made his innovations seem less remarkable.

Paul Was Certain of His Calling

What motivated Paul's novel approach in conveying spiritual truth to the masses? It could be nothing less than his certainty of such a calling, imparted to him by God through prayer, fasting, meditation, studying the Scriptures and direct revelation. In other words, Paul defined the new frontier of ministry in A.D. 40 in obedience to the vision God entrusted to him.

If that vision had been awarded to anybody less intense and less committed, the Church might be different today. Our omniscient

God, knowing our hearts and characters and being aware of how we handle opportunities, chose Paul for that which became the foundational ministry of the age.

Paul is also the example par excellence of the value of vision enabling us to persevere in the face of harsh opposition to God's desires. Like Jesus Himself, the sole explanation for Paul's tenacity is that he was either a lunatic or a fanatic.

History confirms that Paul was a fanatical follower of Christ, one willing to endure whippings, beatings, stonings, shipwrecks, homelessness, muggings, sleeplessness, hunger, thirst, nakedness, robbery, deceit, slander and disloyalty, all for one reason: to serve Jesus Christ with passion and integrity (see 2 Cor. 11:23-28).

A Role for Fanatics

The example Paul gives us underscores a vital truth: Christian visionaries are, by definition, fanatics. Perhaps in the eyes of the world, which prefers those who can be manipulated and controlled, fanatics are dangerous and undesirable. In the eyes of God, though, if a person's zeal is based upon total commitment to the calling of God, fanaticism is the only acceptable lifestyle.

God has no room in His kingdom for the lukewarm individual, the person who lacks passion and urgency in his or her service to God. True visionaries are never lukewarm.

Paul was the quintessential visionary believer. The only love I know that compels bravery and foolishness such as he exhibited is the love for Christ. The only means of translating such love into tangible action is through absolute devotion to His special calling upon us— that is, the realization of His vision for your life and mine.

A Glimpse at Vision

Where can we learn how the Bible's visionaries defined God's vision for their lives? Here are a few of the verses that portray the vision of several key people encountered in the Bible.

Person	Vision	Scripture
Abraham	To lead the Israelites to live in total obedience to God, leading them to a new land prepared for them, toward building a moral community based on unswerving devotion to God alone, while being a blessing to all other people.	Gen. 12:1-3; 13:15; 15:18

Person	Vision	Scripture
Moses	To deliver the Israelites from oppression by leading them to a superior Promised Land while establishing a code of conduct the people may follow to please God.	Exod. 3:7-10; Deut. 26:16-19
Joshua	To conquer and settle the Promised Land, through military victory, based on strategic decisions by God and moral obedience to God's law.	Josh. 1:1-9
Josiah	To restore the God of Israel to the throne of people's hearts, destroying all vestiges of idolatry, restoring the Temple and instituting a reign of justice and righteousness.	2 Kings 23:21-25
Nehemiah	To rally the people of Israel to rebuild the walls and gates of Jerusalem, toward facilitating religious reforms and the spiritual revival of the Jews.	Neh. 2:17; 9:1-3
Peter	To evangelize the Jews in Jerusalem and to create a community of faith that lives by the core principles taught by Jesus and experienced during His ministry by His apostles.	1 Pet. 2:11, 12; 4:12-15
Paul	To evangelize, organize and nurture the Gentiles in the Christian faith, initiating new churches of converts throughout the Roman Empire, encouraging the new believers to reproduce themselves spiritually.	Rom. 15:16-20; Gal. 2:7-10; Eph. 3:7-12
Jesus	To bring salvation, by grace, to the Jews and to enable them to know, love and serve God with all their hearts, minds and souls, and to love other people as themselves.	Matt. 15:24; 22:37-39

Irreplaceable Individuals

You may choose to ignore the lessons provided through the lives of the visionary characters described in Scripture, but to write off their motivations and their gusto is to deny one of the most important lessons God seeks to convey to you.

Could God have used other people to create and develop His Church as He desired? Certainly. He specifically chose these people because of the distinctive qualities they brought to the process. Without their idiosyncratic imprints on the Early Church, the Christian faith would be different today in some discernible and significant ways.

Furthermore, the insights we have about the character of the authentic and impassioned devotee of God would also be significantly different.

A Lesson for Modern People

The example of faith-based vision implemented to the extreme is one of the great lessons from Scripture for modern people. No matter how cultural circumstances change and no matter how church traditions evolve, the timeless truths in the Bible transcend culture and traditions. The centrality of total devotion to Christ and to seeking His mind for the significant ways each of us may serve Him to our utmost ability is one such lesson.

It is not just the heroes of the Bible whose visions have impacted the world for Christ. Many people who are leaders within the Christian community today are visionaries on the same scale as were Peter, Moses or Joshua. Among them are names that might be familiar to you; their familiarity is a direct result of commitment to God's vision.

• *Pat Robertson* reshaped Christian television from being a parade of church services and talking heads to a medium of entertainment, information and teaching founded on biblical principles. Pat's vision for Regent University to produce topflight professionals in industries that significantly influence our culture (such as the media, law and business) is further testimony to his visionary status.

• *Chuck Colson* used his experience in prison to establish a highly regarded international prison ministry. The visionary influence of Colson is most evident through Prison Fellowship's commitment to leading the way in the reconceptualization of the meaning of "criminal justice" and to provide a context for thinking about the notions of truth, justice, fairness, forgiveness and community.

• *Bill Hybels* began a church for the unchurched—Willow Creek Community Church—which contextualized its ministry for the sake of the unchurched without compromising any of the beliefs that make the Christian Church viable. The "seeker-sensitive" ministry approach is now being studied in seminaries and has been implemented in thousands of churches across the world, enabling thousands of irreligious people to become connected to God.

• *James Dobson*, after a successful career in pediatrics, was convinced that the family is the basic building block of society and that when the biblical prescription for family development is tampered with, disastrous results are inevitable. Through Focus on the Family, he has taken the platform as an articulate spokesman for the family and has engineered an extensive web of services, all designed to encourage the Church and families and to protect the family from harmful cultural and governmental attacks.

• *Leighton Ford*, after years as a successful crusade evangelist, noticed the dearth of evangelistic leaders emerging from the Christian community. After a time of soul-searching, he shifted from a primary emphasis upon evangelism to develop a systematic and strategic means of identifying, developing and supporting a forthcoming generation of leaders in evangelism.

• *John Perkins* worked for decades within the African-American community, and experienced the crushing blows of poverty and prejudice. He concluded that many of the obstacles to black people emerging as a proud and self-sufficient race were attributable to a lack of focus on intelligently and strategically applying available resources toward realistic community development. He initiated the Christian Community Redevelopment Association to help conceptualize plans and apply methods for optimizing economic resources of the African-American community.

65

• *David Hubbard*, during his presidency at Fuller Theological Seminary, led in establishing satellite campuses and learning centers as a means of bringing quality seminary education to church leaders who could not afford the time or the expense of relocating for an extended time to attend Fuller's Southern California campus. Seminary training had typically been viewed as an extension of the traditional academic experience: several years of classroom-focused efforts occurring on a sequestered campus, apart from the real world in which ministry happens.

The list of modern visionaries could continue for many pages. You may have bones to pick with the ways some of these people are pursuing the vision God has given them. I encourage you, however, to recognize the tremendous service they perform for the Body of Christ simply through their willingness to devote themselves wholeheartedly to His cause and to His calling.

It is a natural tendency to want to pass judgment on visionaries because they are lightning rods for public emotions. As fellow believers, however, our response ought to be one of admiration and appreciation for their willingness to sell out to Christ's purposes and a sense of awe at God's ability to work in miraculous ways through mere human beings.

Don't overlook the bottom line: God has an army of visionary leaders at work on His behalf throughout the nation. You may read the newspaper or listen to the news and feel discouraged, but never forget that God is at work through thousands of visionaries He has planted in our midst.

New-Era Visionaries

What about the future? Is the Christian community prepared to raise up, release and support a new generation of visionaries who will play a significant role in shaping the new world?

> THE TIME IS RIPE FOR A NEW CLASS OF SPIRITUAL LEADERS TO CAST THE VISION GOD HAS GIVEN THEM FOR THE COMING YEARS. WE ARE ENTERING A MOMENT IN HISTORY WHEN A GENERATION OF GODLY, VISIONARY LEADERS IS READY TO PASS THE TORCH.

Time to Pass the Torch
The time is ripe for a new class of spiritual leaders to cast the vision God has given them for the coming years. We are entering a moment in history when a generation of godly, visionary leaders is ready to pass the torch.

Champions of the faith such as Billy Graham, Bill Bright, John Perkins, Carl Henry, Billy Ray Hearn, Howard Hendricks, Kenneth Taylor—men who have articulated portions of His vision for decades—are still serving the Body, but with diminishing energy as they move into their sunset years. Is it reasonable for us to expect a new corps of leaders to emerge, a group of visionaries God has been quietly preparing to lead us into the third millennium?

God Always Supplies Leaders
You don't have to be a history buff to realize that God never leaves

His people without leaders who are dedicated to His vision for humanity. We would be exhibiting an unbecoming dearth of faith if we did not expect to see a new team of God's chosen ones move to the forefront to articulate and to implement a wealth of exciting, appropriate and complementary visions that will carry us into the new age.

You probably can detect the emergence of a few of those visionaries already. Some of the important visionaries are not household names yet, but they will be in the years to come. Others are already gaining attention for the power of their vision and the blessings bestowed on their efforts by God.

For example, *Bill McCartney*, the college football coach, walked out at the height of a successful career in response to God's call to challenge men to reach their spiritual potential and to address their spiritual responsibility through the Promise Keepers ministry.

John Dawson, a native of New Zealand, travels the world in the quest of biblical reconciliation among people groups who are at odds with each other, such as Caucasians and African-Americans in the United States.

Bob Buford is another visionary, a successful cable television executive who has turned his attention and resources to help churches grow into effective ministry centers, focusing on sharing knowledge, relationships and tangible resources to develop strong congregations.

These men are only three examples of the leaders whose God-given vision for the future is beginning to pay serious dividends for God's kingdom. Many other men and women are stepping into the leadership limelight as well, thrust there not because of their natural talents or egos, but because of their commitments to God's vision.

You must ask yourself some pointed questions about that transition. Does God have a special vision for your life and ministry? What are you doing to clarify that vision, to articulate it and to make it real? And what is your responsibility to others who are called to fulfill God's vision in their lives?

You Will Never Be the Same

When a person discerns God's vision and commits to fulfilling that vision, he or she will never be the same. The person's views about every aspect of life will change, including people's perceptions, the role of faith in daily efforts, how material and intangible resources are used and the definition of success.

God's vision is meant to change you and the world in which you pursue that vision. Remember, turning vision into action creates a new reality. As a person of vision, you are doing more than simply being obedient to God. You are becoming partners with Him in revolutionizing the human experience. You are serving in His army to change the course of human history. You have the privilege of exerting influence in unfolding world events and you have the honor of playing a role in unfurling God's great plan for His creation.

The Face of a Revolutionary?
Maybe you are looking in the mirror and saying, "This sure doesn't look like the face of a revolutionary." Maybe you are thinking you don't have the courage, or the intelligence or the talent to be a force of seminal change in the world.

If you are like most of us, you love to read the stories of David and Paul, but you struggle to envision yourself in their shoes. Sure, you accept the notion that God can use you, but not as a world-shaping leader who will go down in history as a hero of the faith.

Don't Close the Door
Most of us don't think we are capable of being used by God in a dramatic, high-profile manner. Don't close the door on God just yet! Just as He has called you to faith in Christ, so He has called you to His service, based on what you are able to do with His empowerment.

Maybe you won't be the next King David or the apostle Paul of the twenty-first century. That remains to be seen. Even if you are not a servant of that magnitude, your Father in heaven is still counting on you to rise to the occasion and to use your individual abilities to serve Him in ways that are important and special to you. The challenge is not to become a historical figure, but to become a person of relentless faith.

Are you willing to pursue God's vision for you?

Note
1. In this book, I use the word "vision" in a way that is distinct from the traditional biblical usage of "visions." When the Bible speaks of "visions," it typically refers to a mental image that God implants in the mind of the believer for a specific situation. The Bible discusses how prophets had visions, which they then communicated to the people as a means of warning or instructing them. Generally, the visions provided in the Old Testament (where most of those visions are to be found) are meant to be used as a teaching tool to generate a greater degree of righteousness among the people. In this book, however, I use the singular form of the word—vision—as a depiction of a future condition to which we are to dedicate ourselves. God conveys the vision to us through a variety of means, one of which may be a dreamlike vision, but which is not limited to that medium.

CHAPTER

4

Learning the Lessons

"ONE PERSON WITH A BELIEF IS EQUAL
TO A FORCE OF NINETY-NINE WHO ONLY
HAVE AN INTEREST."
—JOHN STUART MILL

Who would have imagined that we could find common ground between the apostle Paul, the man who preached sexual and moral purity, and Alfred Kinsey, the high priest of sexual and moral anarchy?

Had you ever thought about the overlap in the lives of Dr. Benjamin Spock, who devoted his life to caring for children, and King Solomon, who fathered hundreds of them?

Isn't it ironic that there is a core similarity between William Levitt, who built homes for thousands, and Moses, who took thousands away from their homes?

All these people have one thing in common: They were compelled by vision. In most cases, the similarities end there. One group pursued their personal vision for the future; the other group was driven by God's vision for the future.

The fulfillment achieved by those who chased their own vision ranged from negligible to substantial; yet, the degree of satisfaction achieved by God's emissaries seems consistently complete.

If we concentrate on the lessons we can learn from godly visionaries, we can save ourselves from the brutality of discovery-by-trial-and-error. Experience may be the best teacher, as some have suggested, but it is also the costliest. The trial-and-error approach consumes enormous and, usually, unnecessary amounts of time, energy, resources and emotions.

The Bible provides for us accounts of the experiences and outcomes of God's chosen visionaries to save us from the pain and poor stewardship of having to reinvent the process.

I have learned 18 lessons by studying the lives of biblical visionaries. These lessons are relevant to all Christians, in all walks of life and in all periods of human history. They may be broken into four kinds: (1) the demands of visionary living, (2) the character of God's vision, (3) the people's response to the vision and (4) the visionary's experience with the vision.

The Demands of God's Vision

Vision Requires Change
Vision is God's means of motivating people to grow closer to Him. Abraham encouraged his extended family and servants to leave their

> PAUL WAS A SOCIAL CLIMBER IN THE RANKS OF THE RELIGIOUS LEADERS, BUT HIS ENCOUNTER WITH GOD TAUGHT HIM THAT SUCCESS WAS NOT BASED ON ROUTINE, TRADITION, CONTACTS, FORENSIC SKILL OR INTELLIGENCE.

homes and to join him on a journey to a new place and a new way of life.

Moses had to surrender the comfortable life of a prince to become the leader of an ill-mannered troop of vagabonds wandering in the desert.

Josiah pioneered many changes in the lifestyle and values of the nation because it was God's desire that Israel live differently.

Nehemiah championed to rebuild Jerusalem, but ultimately led the people of Israel to redevelopment, tasks that demanded sacrifice, relocation, strenuous labor and physical risks—change, change, change.

We will never amount to much if we are satisfied with who we are today. God places irritants in our midst—we call them visionaries—who drive us to become more Christlike and more devoted to His objectives rather than to our own.

Change is hard to embrace because it pushes us into the unknown. Progress and meaning are achieved, however, only when we take risks and seek growth. Vision can direct our paths to meaningful growth, but only if we are open to change.

Vision Redefines Success

Abraham was successful until God showed him that material wealth was poverty in eternity. Moses had it made as the adopted son of the Egyptian pharaoh, but he discovered that the finest clothing, the best education and a daily regimen of well-prepared meals were meaningless unless life was devoted to God's desires. Paul was a social climber in the ranks of the religious leaders, but his encounter with God taught him that success was not based on routine, tradition, contacts, forensic skill or intelligence.

God's vision defines success as radical obedience to His special direction for your life. Each of us has a different but equally important vision from our Master. He is less concerned with what you are capable of accomplishing for Him than He is with your passion and commitment in pursuing the vision (see Ps. 25; Prov. 3:5,6; Jer. 29:11-13; Eph. 2:10).

Ultimately, God's set of goals must be sought, not the desires of your heart or the fruits of your natural abilities, even if the intent is to please Him. He inevitably uses the unusual mixture of experiences, abilities and gifts you possess, using you in your areas of strength so that you do not fail if your heart is devoted to pure, God-directed service.

Vision Demands Perseverance

Have you ever wondered how many times Moses must have listened to his legion of whiners and felt like abandoning the whole pack, right in the middle of the desert? Do you ever imagine yourself in Paul's shoes and conclude that it would be a lot easier and more intelligent to set up camp with his itinerant team and simply conduct Bible studies each night around the campfire?

I have often marveled at David's ability to persevere in the face of challenges. Wouldn't it have made more sense to offer a royal decree about moral living, to appoint a few good teachers of the Scriptures to oversee the worship in the Temple and then to retire to a fabulous palace on the mountainside while he was still young enough to enjoy his favored circumstances?

The heroes of vision teach us that God blesses them in ways that are not of the world and that their blessings are perhaps related to their determination to persevere. Because the Bible teaches us that

God will not give us more than we can handle when we are seeking to do His work, diligence in the face of oppression and hardship are hallmarks of true vision (see 2 Cor. 10:13; Phil. 2:13).

What empowers the person to persevere during stress and opposition? A pure love of God, love that is so grateful for being counted worthy to serve Him that enduring trials and tribulations seems like nothing more than a temporary nuisance.

That is surely what compelled Paul to keep on track (see 1 Tim. 1:12-17). This intense love of God and thankfulness for His calling is certainly behind the efforts of Abraham. No doubt, Joshua was eager to go to battle against better-trained, better-armed, bigger armies of the Canaanites because he had total belief that God had called him and therefore would supply whatever he needed to bring about God's objectives.

Vision without perseverance is like an interesting chapter in an unfinished book. It neither pleases the author (you), the audience (the world who should have benefited from the vision) or the publisher (God) who commissioned the book.

Vision Requires Hard Work

Nehemiah led the people in the back-breaking task of clearing, cutting, placing and securing thousands of tons of stone and lumber to complete the initial portion of the vision. Peter spent years striving to lead the new church—based in Jerusalem—to spiritual maturity, using all his abilities and gifts to orchestrate the growth (see Neh. 1—13; Acts 1:5,8; 9:32—12).

Moses' leadership stretched his personal abilities and his physical stamina, finally experiencing relief when his father-in-law offered some management advice (see Exod. 18:1-27). Josiah spent three decades undoing what those before him had worked hard to do, working on the minds and the hearts of the people, before they would revert again to evildoing (see 2 Kings 22—23; 2 Chron. 34—35).

Some people think of vision as a process of dreaming, then ordering people around until the dream comes to pass. No biblical evidence supports such behavior. Evidence does suggest, however, that vision is a holistic process in which the visionary articulates the vision and becomes intimately involved in applying the vision to the world's conditions.

Vision is hard work because it requires change and growth. God's vision is not geared to the incremental enhancement of circumstances; it embraces wholesale redevelopment. Implementing vision is never easy.

Analysis Helps Provide Context

God does not give us His vision until we have taken the time and made the effort to understand its context. Nehemiah needed a firm grasp of the condition of Jerusalem to spark the vision in his mind. Paul required meetings with some of the saints and an extended time in prayer, reflection and deliberation before the pieces fit.

Joshua, like his mentor Moses, used strategic intelligence gatherers (i.e., spies) to give him a more complete sense of how the vision might be implemented. Paul had a consistent process of information dissemination—incoming and outgoing letters, constant conversations with traveling Christians who could provide updates on his churches and converts—to help him evaluate the state of the vision.

You serve a logical God. His universe is orderly and He works in an orderly fashion. He expects you to operate in an orderly manner as well. Analyzing information about your environment is one means by which you can determine how to effectively implement the vision.

The Character of God's Vision

Vision Will Threaten Your Comfort Zone
Vision ultimately results in a superior life for those who buy into the vision. For those who carry the message and seek to bring it to fruition, resistance is par for the course. Paul was stoned, beaten, demeaned and jailed. Abraham was mocked. Moses had to endure complaints from within his camp and military threats from without, all because of his commitment to God's vision.

73

No matter who you are and no matter what your personal abilities and spiritual gifts may be, implementing God's vision will become controversial because it rips people out of their comfort zones. This may perturb you, but it is not a vital concern to the God who gave you the vision. After all, from His point of view, vision is not about delivering an easier lifestyle; it is about obedience to His will, toward seeing His goals being fulfilled.

If you are eager to discover His vision so that life will become easier, prepare for extreme disappointment. Vision is always accompanied by anguish, confrontation and skepticism. If you have cast the vision to others and find that everyone is perfectly amenable to it, one of three conditions exists: you haven't cast God's vision, they didn't understand what you said or you don't know how to read the audience.

Vision Is Not Easily Embraced by Others
In a postmodern, secularized culture, God's vision appears foolish. Living for eternity runs counter to society's "grab all of the gusto"

approach to living for self and for the moment. Even those people who, at some stage, break through the worldly hype and grasp His vision may not remain true zealots in the battle to see the vision become reality.

The vision must constantly be retold and resold. This truism is illustrated in the life of Josiah, who was personally devoted to a vision. Because he did not sufficiently reinforce the vision among the people, his death brought a return to the wicked ways of the past and

> IT IS A FUNCTION OF THE VISIONARY TO SUSTAIN
> PEOPLE'S PASSION FOR THE VISION. THE FAILURE
> TO DO SO REFLECTS AS MUCH ON THE VISIONARY AS
> ON THE PEOPLE WHO HAVE DEPARTED FROM THE VISION.

a dismissal of the efforts made during Josiah's reign to bring the vision to fruition. The people loved Josiah, but they did not love the vision promulgated by their young king.

Nehemiah struggled with some people who failed to see beyond the reconstructed buildings and to recognize the related need for reconstructed lives. Joshua was a great and righteous man, but his people remained impure in their worship.

Each of these people had the sacred privilege of leading others to apply God's vision. Each, in his own way, discovered that it takes a perpetual campaign of restating the vision, reinforcing its significance and rewarding people for their loyalty to the vision.

For some people, the vision becomes a temporary cause. It is a function of the visionary, however, to sustain people's passion for the vision. The failure to do so reflects as much on the visionary as on the people who have departed from the vision.

Vision Unfolds Progressively

Although biblical visionaries clearly understood the heart of the vision from the beginning, the details may have come into sharper focus as events transpired.

Moses and Joshua—the desert commandos—are examples of how the vision progressively came into focus. They knew they were on a journey to a Promised Land, but they were not sure of where, how long it would take, what they might have to do once they arrived or the nature of the land itself.

Thus, as Joshua entered the land, he had to use military strategy and competence to clear the land of trespassers. Josiah knew that the heart of the vision was to restore purity of worship and justice to the land, but it wasn't until the discovery of the Book of the Covenant that some of the most significant reforms took place.

Nehemiah had done a great work in rebuilding the holy city, but the struggle was reconstructing the hearts of the people—a task he was not fully prepared to undertake until the bricks and mortar redevelopment was well under way.

Sometimes God protects us from our own fears and anxieties by not allowing us to fully understand the vision. If you take the step of faith of pursuing the vision, He will reveal enough of that vision so you know which direction to pursue and the ultimate goals you are striving to achieve. Be prepared, though, for new revelations along the path, insights that will clarify and better focus your energies on outcomes that are truly miraculous.

Vision Is Entrusted to an Individual

Did you notice in the Bible that God never gave vision to a committee? In every case, God selected a person for whom He tailored a vision for a better future. No person in Scripture was entrusted with the entire vision for the re-creation and perfection of humanity; each visionary is given a small portion of God's aggregate plan for the future of the world.

75

People may play a role in your comprehension of the special vision God has for you, but they cannot tell you the vision nor certify that your articulation of the vision is accurate and appropriate.

God's vision is a matter of direct conversation between you and Him, just as your fulfillment of that vision is a matter of evaluation between the two of you. God does not need a group to discern His will for an individual. If you are in proper relation with Him, neither do you.

Vision Is an Adventure

In our results-oriented society, we often judge performance on the basis of meeting deadlines, staying within budgets and producing the expected outcomes. A careful examination of the ways God works with those who carry forth His vision, however, shows that the journey is just as important as the ultimate destination. In other words, He is every bit as interested in how we act, how we change and what we experience in the process of pursuing His vision as He is in seeing us reach the objective.

Take a look at Abraham and his fellow sojourners. What happened to them as they made their way to their new residence was the heart of the transformation in which God was keenly interested.

Reaching the new land was not as significant to God as the challenges and changes that redefined Abraham's commitment to Yahweh.

Moses is another great example of the significance of the journey. His life cannot be judged a failure because he was not allowed to enter into the long-awaited promised turf. Do you think God's evaluation of Moses is based solely upon the fact that Moses disqualified himself from setting foot on the new territory or on the basis of how Moses changed from a haughty murderer to a hot-tempered leader of a contentious people to a true leader of men and lover of God?

God uses vision as one of the mechanisms by which He shapes us into the usable servants He clearly wants us to become.

Vision Outlives the Visionary

There is a difference between goals, strategy and vision. Goals and strategies are short-term outcomes that we may achieve. Vision is the result of long-term effort.

Moses lived a long life. It was not long enough, however, to watch his people set foot on the land God had promised. The vision was accomplished by Joshua, his trusted lieutenant.

The other side of the coin is represented by Josiah. The vision God entrusted to that revered king was not fully accomplished during Josiah's prematurely ended lifetime. The vision outlived Josiah. Sadly, he did not have a Joshua to whom he could pass the torch; consequently, the vision was blurred, then lost. If Josiah had lived longer, perhaps God would have enabled him to see the vision completed. But he didn't, and it wasn't. The vision not only outlived the visionary, but also died for lack of a visionary who could champion it past the death of the initial recipient.

Our timing and our ways of measuring success are not those of the Lord. We like to see things resolved and completed, everything neat and predictable, well defined and on schedule. God operates on a different timetable and has reasons we will never know or comprehend (see Deut. 29:29; Isa. 55:8,9).

It is sufficient for us to realize that the vision God gives to one person may be faithfully implemented by one or more successors, following a schedule that only He knows. Again, the operative factor is not achievement, but faithfulness.

Vision Reflects God's Objectives

In the first chapter of this book, we explored human vision and those people who gave their lives to their personal vision for a better future. Of course, even the best efforts of the most intelligent and gifted people did not result in a better tomorrow, because their purposes were not God's purposes.

God plays by different rules and seeks different outcomes than human beings do. He doesn't care about wealth, prestige, innovations, records, posterity or human desires. He cares about holiness and obedience (see Jer. 9:23,24).

Often the ways God helps us to become more righteous are totally different from the ways we might recommend. Sending tens of thousands of people on a 40-year hike through the desert is not a human strategy. Sending a zealous Jew to minister to the non-Jews makes little sense to our minds.

> PEOPLE OF PASSION ARE THE EXCEPTION TO THE RULE IN OUR SOCIETY, AND PEOPLE WHO ARE PASSIONATE ABOUT SPIRITUAL MATTERS ARE DIFFICULT FOR AMERICANS TO UNDERSTAND.

God alone is omniscient; His vision for us is the best possible vision, even if it conflicts with our assumptions, preferences and prayers. All we need to know is that His vision comes with an eternal guarantee that if we obey, He will bless us beyond our wildest dreams, and in ways we might not perceive as significant or as blessings.

77

People's Response to God's Vision

Vision Often Frightens People
Notice one thing about vision: Once you have it and are committed to it, people often brand you a lunatic. They did it with Moses. They did it with Paul. They did it with Jesus. The passion for the vision, the zeal devoted to the vision and the nonworldly nature of the vision scare the daylights out of people.

People of passion are the exception to the rule in our society, and people who are passionate about spiritual matters are difficult for Americans to understand. Be prepared to frighten a few people by your promise to serve only God and to serve Him to the fullest extent of your capabilities. Notions such as dying to self, living for others, eschewing the best the world has to offer and seeking to please God are ideas that have a negative frame of reference for millions of contemporary Americans (see Mark 8:34-38).

Vision Motivates the Masses

Say what you will about the inadequacies of biblical visionaries, you must acknowledge that something in their lives caused each of them to attract a substantial following. Moses was not a good public speaker, but thousands of people followed him on a dangerous and ill-defined path. Josiah was just a boy, yet an entire nation altered its customs and lifestyles to accommodate his passion. David was a shepherd and a man on the run from a king, yet he became the greatest king of his nation. Paul became such a compelling visionary figure that ancient literature records indicate that he was growing his own cult. Peter had been unable to lead the Twelve during the time of Christ, yet after His death and resurrection, Peter was able to bring together thousands of people for productive and significant purposes.

The fact that a vision can excite people speaks to our inner yearning to lead lives of significance. God's vision enables us to enlist people's assistance and to empower them toward the fruition of the vision in spite of our own lack of charisma, abilities or experience. The visionary does not need natural gifts, only a heart of commitment.

The Visionary's Response to God's Vision

Vision Breaks Your Heart

God's vision relates to things that matter to us. As a result, the visionary often is overwhelmed emotionally when considering the transformation needed to counter the world in which we live.

The best example of this is Nehemiah. When he learned that the walls of Jerusalem were still in ruins, he immediately cried, fasted and prayed. This process continued for days. The situation was so poignant to him that it broke his heart. His demeanor changed, his life ceased to have meaning and his thoughts were drawn to the dilapidation of the capital city of the Jews.

Study the lives of biblical visionaries. God did not yank them out of one circumstance and throw them into something for which they did not have a soft place in their hearts. Quite the opposite. God prepares each of us for a special task that is meaningful to us deep inside.

A vision-based ministry and living will convert the deepest yearnings of your heart into life-changing action that glorifies God and serves humanity. You will know you have captured the true vision when you feel so deeply moved by the possibility of being able to do something about the situation that any other possibilities pale by comparison.

Vision Redefines Personal Ambition

Do you believe that all Moses was capable of accomplishing in life was leading a ragtag band through the desert? Instead of separating the land among the various tribes of Israel, Joshua could just as easily have decided to maintain control of everything they had conquered and become a powerful ruler of the age. Wasn't it absurd for Paul to continually travel to establish new congregations when he could easily have stayed in one place and have built the original megachurch?

The motivation behind the visionary leaders' actions are different from the motivations of other people. In short, the visionary who is serving God ceases to live for personal ambition, but rather for God's ambitions. The things of this world are minor in comparison to the eternal ways and means of God (see 1 John 2:15-17). Living to accomplish His objectives in His ways effectively dissipates the driving ambitions and dreams we may have had before becoming infected with His vision.

Vision Instills Humility

If you discover God's vision for your life, it will humble you (see 1 Pet. 5:5,6). It humbled Abraham so much that he was constantly building altars and worshiping God. It humbled Moses, whose congenitally combative personality was softened by recognizing the privilege God entrusted to him. It also humbled Paul, the religious yuppie of his day. Paul often referred to himself in humble terms, such as "I am the least of the apostles" (1 Cor. 15:9) and "I am less than the least of all God's people" (Eph. 3:8).

What instigates such humility among people who receive such a magnificent task? They recognize that they are neither worthy nor capable of handling that magnificent task, yet the task was awarded to them just the same by an all-knowing and perfect God. The Scriptures indicate that the more experienced the person becomes in the pursuit of the vision, the more humble he or she becomes.

Vision Drives Us to God

Not the least of the principles emerging from our study of biblical visionaries is that vision drives us into a closer harmony with God. Notice how often the visionaries go to their knees in prayer. Take note of the number of times these individuals stopped everything they were doing to worship God. Don't overlook the expressions of the need for holiness and righteousness.

God's vision is a remarkable challenge and an indescribable blessing. It is given only to those who can be trusted with it and to those who will be fully committed to it. Our abilities and experiences have little to do with God's determination to bless us with His vision; for vision is a matter of the heart, not a matter of competence (see 2 Cor. 12:9).

We are all incompetent to accomplish the vision He provides for us. We qualify as candidates, however, when we acknowledge this inadequacy and determine to live in absolute obedience to the vision.

Principles Learned from Biblical Visionaries

The Demands of God's Vision
1. It requires change.
2. It redefines success.
3. It demands perseverance.
4. It requires hard work.
5. It is consistent with environmental analysis.

The Character of God's Vision
6. It is not comfortable.
7. It is not easily embraced by others.
8. It unfolds progressively.
9. It is entrusted to an individual.
10. It is as much a journey as it is a destination.
11. It outlives the visionary.
12. It reflects God's objectives.

People's Response to God's Vision
13. It frightens people.
14. It motivates the masses.

The Visionary's Response to God's Vision
15. It breaks your heart.
16. It redefines personal ambition.
17. It instills humility.
18. It drives us to God.

CHAPTER 5

The Visionary Hierarchy

"SOME MEN SEE THINGS AS THEY ARE AND
ASK 'WHY?' I DREAM OF THINGS THAT
NEVER WERE AND ASK 'WHY NOT?'"
—GEORGE BERNARD SHAW

During an international evangelistic meeting, I blamed visionless leaders for the plight of the church in America. Later, a member of the audience took offense, contending that vision is reserved for a chosen few.

Although my research has led me to a different conclusion from that of my critic, perhaps we can eliminate the confusion by noting that visionaries generally fit into one of three categories that form a hierarchy of vision: micro, mezzo and macro.

Three-Part Harmony

One of the basic principles we find in Scripture is that God tests us with degrees of responsibility. To those people who prove faithful,

He entrusts greater responsibility. Other people cannot handle additional responsibility. In some ways, you might say that God was the originator of the Peter Principle (i.e., people work their way up to their levels of incompetence).

Look at the Christian community today. Some believers struggle to make vision the guiding principle in their lives. Their focus is not on changing the world, the nation or the city for Christ. Their emphasis focuses on being faithful servants in their families, at work and with their friends. Adam, Noah, Aaron, Job, Martha and Ruth are a few of the Bible characters who fit this level of vision.

THE VISION-GIVING PROCESS IS ONE IN WHICH GOD WILL GRANT US AS MUCH VISION AS HE CAN TRUST US TO PURSUE WITH IMAGINATION, ENERGY, PASSION AND DILIGENCE.

You probably know people who have moved beyond vision that only influences their immediate network of relationships and experiences. They have been given a broader vision for a church, a community, a state and a region.

Such people often occupy positions in ministry, government or business that allow them to apply their vision to an expanded territory, to touch a greater number of lives. Pastors are generally included in this category. So, too, are missionaries and many church elders. Isaac, Jonathan, Jethro, Deborah, Peter and Luke fit this mold as well.

The upper end of the continuum are those people we sometimes, in our less genteel moments, think of as the overachievers. We often refer to them as "driven." All too often, that term is used in a pejorative way rather than to celebrate the fact that they may be driven by God's vision.

These are the high-profile, public people whose vision touches a nation or beyond. These are the global players, people who are definitely in the "major leagues" of ministry, government and business. International evangelists, parachurch ministry founders and pastors of outreach-oriented megachurches often have this breadth of vision. So, too, did Abraham, David, Moses, Joshua, Gideon, Nehemiah and Paul.

This three-part harmony of gifted believers is no accident. God intentionally challenges us to move from the lowest to the greatest in terms of how much of His vision we can handle effectively (see Luke

16:10). The vision-giving process is one in which God will grant us as much vision as He can trust us to pursue with imagination, energy, passion and diligence.

Let's consider the three levels in more detail. Those people on the lower end of the continuum are micro-visionaries. Those who graduate to the middle level are the mezzo-visionaries. Those who reach the top are the macro-visionaries.

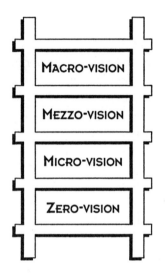

Micro-Visionaries

My friend Mike is a micro-visionary. He has been a Christian for more than 20 years. He loves Christ and wants to be counted among the good and faithful servants. He regularly attends church services with his wife and child. He reads the Bible regularly. He prays daily. He listens occasionally to Christian radio. He earns a good living and his family lives comfortably.

Mike has no illusions about his ability to change the world for Christ in any dramatic ways. He is convinced that if he can do the basics of the faith—be faithful in his marriage, pay his taxes without cheating the government, respect his parents, live a clean life and so on—he is maximizing his ability to serve God.

His vision is to use his average talents to create an environment of trust with a few non-Christian friends toward eventually having an opportunity to share Christ with them in a soft sell approach.

Mike's vision is comparatively limited. He relates God's vision for his life and personal ministry to the immediate needs of his family, to the relationships he has on the job and to how he interacts with the people he knows at his church. When Mike thinks about how he can shape the future in relation to God's desires, he thinks of the small circle of people he knows personally.

He thinks about the experiences he has had, the talent he possesses, the spiritual gift he believes he has and then dreams of how he can draw on these tangible or assumed resources and apply them.

I am not in any way demeaning Mike's position as a micro-visionary. I thank God for his friendship and for his undiminished desire to serve Christ in whatever ways are feasible for him. Someday he may become a mezzo-visionary. In any event, he is part of God's eternal family and is valued by God as much as any mezzo-visionary or macro-visionary you can name.

Every Christian is called to be, at the very least, a micro-visionary. No believer can create a legitimate excuse for not having a sufficient measure of God's vision to leave some mark on the world he or she touches daily. The vision may be finite and restricted, but just as the Body of Christ needs people who have various gifts operating in cooperation and harmony to reach a global audience, the Church needs a broad-based foundation of micro-visionaries to influence their more limited but equally important worlds.

In all probability, each of us begins the Christian life as a micro-visionary. Some graduate to greater vision; most don't. Whether the failure to ascend to a higher level on the vision hierarchy is by God's design or our own incompetence or complacency remains to be seen.

You and I need to be supportive of micro-visionaries. Our churches are built on them. The reason churches don't make a dent in the postmodern culture is not that they have too many micro-visionaries. It is because they are weighed down with too many Christians—a majority—who have no vision whatsoever. Becoming a micro-visionary would be a major step up and a blessing to God, to their churches, to their families, to their friends and to themselves.

Yes, "micro" means small; but it is better to have a person of small vision who faithfully and effectively executes that faith than to have a million people who attend church regularly, but never pursue God's vision. May God grant us more micro-visionaries in the days ahead.

Mezzo-Visionaries

"Mezzo" (pronounced met-so) is the Italian term for "in the middle." Mezzo-visionaries are those people who are in intermediary phases of ministry and perspective. They have proven their abilities to implement vision in the most intimate circumstances—families, work, churches, neighborhoods—and are ready to tackle bigger challenges. God is only too happy to use them in this way.

In moving beyond personal vision, the mezzo-visionary embraces a vision for wider influence. The vision may relate to a type of ministry; it might relate to a challenge to one aspect of the culture; it could pertain to a particular group of people to be influenced in a unique manner.

You probably know a handful of mezzo-visionaries. They are generally people who rise to positions of leadership within the local church because these are people God is blessing and who are driven for a bigger ministry purpose. They are not perfect; they are just expanding the influence of the Church through their heightened ability to discern, own and apply a bigger vision.

Macro-Visionaries

Having mastered micro and mezzo-vision, these rare individuals are the best-known servants of God because they cast a global vision for the Church's consideration and peripheral involvement.

These are the people we typically view as major Christian leaders. People such as Chuck Colson, Bill Hybels, Ron Sider, Bill Bright, Pat Robertson and Billy Graham are a few of the names you would expect to find in the directory of macro-visionaries.

> MACRO-VISIONARIES GENERALLY HAVE COME UP THROUGH THE RANKS, GRADUATING FROM MICRO-VISION TO MEZZO-VISION BEFORE THEY WERE PERMITTED TO SERVE AS MACRO-VISIONARIES.

85

Often you find that the macro-visionaries have lived through many trials and tribulations. The most impressive thing about them, however, is not the size of the dream, but the intensity of their pursuit of that God-inspired dream. Macro-visionaries generally have come up through the ranks, graduating from micro-vision to mezzo-vision before they were permitted to serve as macro-visionaries.

One of the responsibilities these special individuals have is to identify high-potential people whose vision capacity can be stretched so that they, too, can join the ranks of the macro-visionaries. The existing macro-visionaries, then, have sacred duties to mentor potential macro-visionaries.

The Challenge

If people are not born into macro-level vision, but must work their way to such levels of responsibility, what does that say to you?

The following are some of the questions this realization raised for me:

- What is my heart's desire: to resist pressure and challenges and live at the micro-vision level or to seek to accomplish great things for God to the boundaries of my capabilities and thus become a macro-visionary?
- What am I doing to learn the lessons of my current level and to prepare for graduation to the next?
- Who are the role models to whom I gravitate and what level of aspirations and ability will a close study of their lives plant within me?
- For those who are not as mature as I am in vision, but who clearly desire to reach their maximum level of vision development, in what ways can I assist in their development?
- What are the obstacles present in my life, right now, that could prevent me, or could disqualify me, from graduating to the next level of visionary living?
- What is the price I must pay for moving to the next level of vision? Am I ready to pay that price?
- Am I capable of stepping to the next level, or should I be satisfied that God has brought me to a level that will continue during the duration of my life?

I believe vision contains some parallels with teaching. In James 3:1, we are told that we should seek great respect for that responsibility, recognizing that because of their influence, teachers will be judged by a higher standard.

I believe that visionaries, too, will be held accountable by God in accordance with the degree of trust and responsibility He invests in us, through the vision. Do not take the development and the deployment of God's vision for your life, ministry or church lightly.

Who Receives Vision?

Reflect for a moment on the God you know and love and who knows and loves you even more deeply. Can you imagine God actively and intentionally choosing to not allow a true believer some degree of vision for the future?

Is it consistent with God's character to seek a relationship with a person, but then to deny that person the insight of knowing how to live for the glory of God by producing the greatest influence, efficiency and personal sense of fulfillment?

Does the God you serve play favorites, randomly selecting some people to play significant roles while abandoning others to mediocrity of service?

An Individual Relationship

God loves each of us and wants us to develop an intimate relationship with Him. Part of our love for Him is demonstrated through our com-

> WE SERVE A LOGICAL, ORDERLY GOD,
>
> ONE WHO DOES NOT CALL US TO COMPETE WITH
>
> EACH OTHER, BUT WHO PREPARES US FOR EFFECTIVE
>
> AND COOPERATIVE MINISTRY.

mitment to the Christian life, a vital portion of which relates to service. Because he gives each person different gifts and abilities, divergent experiences and resources, it makes sense that each believer has a different vision to fulfill.

We serve a logical, orderly God, one who does not call us to compete with each other, but who prepares us for effective and cooperative ministry. Vision clarifies, in our minds and hearts, the contours of that service.

Is it possible for a person to be a leader but have no vision? The very idea is absurd! What is a leader? Someone who understands the context, articulates a plan of action and a purpose underlying that action, and then orchestrates the activity necessary to see that plan implemented. If a leader does not have vision, what would he or she lead people toward? "Visionless leader" is an oxymoron.

More than Mere Mission

The plan and the purpose are based on more than mere mission. They are based on vision, the detailed perspective about the future that the leader and his or her followers have been called to create. A person who is labeled "leader" but does not have a clear sense of what he or she is seeking to accomplish is not a leader but a follower, one who is dependent upon the guidance provided by others.

It is possible to have a micro-visionary in a position of leadership. These people struggle with leadership because they have a hard time seeing beyond themselves and their most immediate circumstances. It is possible for a mezzo-visionary or macro-visionary to be a leader and to succeed. Realize, however, that the presence of vision does not guarantee that a person will be an effective leader.

Vision is necessary, but is not a substitute for success in leadership. Effective leadership requires the ability to discern and to articulate vision, the ability to develop a team that will strategize and plan for transformation, the ability to delegate tasks and to encourage others in that endeavor.

The point is that everyone who assumes leadership must have vision.

CHAPTER
6

What Are
Your Values?

"IF YOU DON'T STAND FOR SOMETHING, YOU
FALL FOR ANYTHING."—ANONYMOUS

A 16-year-old boy who confesses to killing an 11-year-old neighbor while high on marijuana is sentenced to 47 years in prison.

A yearlong study of television programming conducted by researchers at four universities concludes that the majority of programs contained some violence and that the context in which that violence occurred can be "psychologically harmful."

A three-year-old girl dies, the victim of what a medical examiner classifies as battered child syndrome.

A former U.S. Senator is sentenced to a year of probation, ending the ethics case in which he admits falsifying his congressional expense account.

The behavior of the subjects featured in the preceding news reports does not represent what most of us consider "traditional values" in our society. More likely, that behavior would be cited as a reason for public concern about such issues as crime, violence in television programming, conduct of public officials, public school philosophies and the religious community's involvement in politics and government.

Despite a growing public interest in such matters, studies by the Barna Research Group show that most adults are at a loss when asked to describe the meaning of values in general or to articulate their own values in particular.

For the visionary, values are an indispensable part of the development process. As noted in chapter 2, values constitute the foundation of God's vision.

It is impossible to receive a vision from God that conflicts with the kinds of values He instructs us to embrace for our lives. Understanding biblical values and developing practical ways of integrating them into our lifestyles represent crucial tasks for committed Christians.

Determining Values

As always, we start with the Bible to identify values. God has not left us clueless when it comes to building a values base. We may appropriate a comprehensive group of values from the life principles described in Scripture.

If values are those elements to which we ascribe worth and are worth adopting as a cornerstone of character, then the Bible represents an archive of instruction about the topic.

As you reflect on the lives of key visionaries in the Bible, you can discern some of the values that drove their thinking and behavior and that helped shape their worldviews and vision. Because values help us in making choices—from the most mundane to life-and-death decisions—we can understand the values of biblical visionaries partly by analyzing the choices they made, especially in times of stress and confrontation.

Christ Serves as a Model
The teachings of Jesus Christ and Paul, in particular, provide clear insights into the kinds of values that define the character of a Christian.

Rather than identify what your values should be, if such a pronouncement is possible, let me state emphatically that determining your values is a necessary and important step in your personal development and maturity as a Christian. Ascertaining those values is also a key step toward becoming a vision-driven believer. Pinpointing your values, however, is a personal matter.

No one can do it for you because you are describing the kind of person you want to be. Similarly, if you are striving to identify the core values of your church, you cannot copy the list of values offered by other churches because those congregations have different personalities, histories, leadership teams and internal cultures.

MISSION GIVES YOUR LIFE PURPOSE.

VISION GIVES YOUR LIFE DIRECTION.

VALUES GIVE YOU CHARACTER.

Mission gives your life purpose. Vision gives your life direction. Values give you character. Until you can identify your values, your character is prone to make dangerous shifts. Values convey who you are: the parameters you have set for yourself in terms of ethical, moral, theological and personal beliefs.

Values Direct Behavior
Until you can confidently state your values, every philosophy, every behavior and every desire known to humankind is a potential substitute. Your values become the filter through which you determine right from wrong, value from worthlessness and importance from insignificance. If you do not specifically identify your values, they will be defined for you by the whims and influences of the world.

Values are the nonnegotiable perspectives in your life. More often than not, people who do not intentionally set forth their values in a clear and precise format waffle under pressure. When it comes to concern about consistency and backbone, Christians who do not have well-defined sets of values run little danger of moral or ethical compromise because people who have no clear values have nothing to compromise.

On the other hand, people who specify their values are more likely to live in harmony with those core beliefs. After you have determined your core values, you can use them for the following purposes:

1. As the basis for consistent and appropriate decisions;
2. As the foundation from which your vision originates;

91

3. As the fundamental precepts to which you may be held accountable by those whom you trust and who care about you;
4. As a filter through which you may judge the importance of opportunities or alternatives;
5. As the baseline for evaluating your growth as a follower of Christ and as a leader in various walks of life;
6. As a practical interpretation of biblical principles about maturity and character.

Know Who You Are

To become a true visionary, you must know who you are. It is unlikely that God will reveal His vision for your life and ministry until you have overtly declared what is important in your character. Until you are willing and are able to articulate those values, your thinking and behavior are liable to be unpredictable and volatile. You have yet to declare your essence.

I encourage you to define your values in the same way you should craft a focused, precise mission statement and vision statement. It is one more way you declare what you stand for and what can be expected of you. On a more personal level, a Christian who knows his or her character is a person at peace with self and the world because the probability of experiencing inconsistencies in thought, word, deed and character have been minimized.

Sources of Values

Suggesting that your values should derive from the Bible, alone, is a bit idealistic or superficial. God's Word is sufficient to guide our lives; but He allows us to learn from experiences, people, prayer and other resources, too.

Hunter Lewis argues that we arrive at our values in any of six ways.[1]

1. *Authority.* Values emerge from cues of an external source of knowledge or perspective you trust. For Christians, the Bible or a trusted pastor are examples of an authority figure you may consult or trust in shaping your values. Experts, such as college professors, government leaders, social activists, religious figures, business leaders and authors, also may influence your thinking about values.
2. *Deductive logic.* This process allows you to examine

prospective values and their consistency with objective and subjective reality. This approach encourages you to state those truths you believe are at the core of your character and to test them logically.

3. *Experience.* You may select some values because you have directly experienced them in your life. As you study your past and determine what has been most important and significant in your life, those experiences that left a lasting impression upon you, or had a major influence upon your life, may become the basis of your values.

4. *Emotion.* Many people identify values based on their feelings. This is distinct from logic, which is intellectual. Often people identify values based on what feels right, good or appropriate.

5. *Intuition.* When you rely upon the unconscious mind to deliver insights, you are leaning on your intuition. This is decision making without reliance upon identifiable, factual reasoning. Some people develop their values on the basis of an intuitive self-perception.

6. *Science.* The scientific method is the most sophisticated, or, at least, the most complicated. It demands that a hypothesis be developed and tested so that a conclusion may be deemed accurate and reliable based on replicable practice and observable results.

The Bible Is the Best Source of Values
It is possible for a Christian to arrive at core values through any of the preceding six methods. Although nobody can tell you what your values should be, I believe it is reasonable to suggest that every Christian gain a sense of values primarily from an authoritative source, most notably, the Bible. The kinds of values you derive from God's Word should form the bedrock of your values, a group of principles, beliefs and perspectives that are central to your life and remain nonnegotiable in your daily experience.

The Bible offers myriad values for your consideration. The following are a few values that are described in Scripture:

Description of the Value	Sources
Love of God above all else	Deut. 5:7-10; Matt 22:37
Love people	Matt. 5:43-47; 22:38; 1 Cor. 12
Forgiveness	Matt. 5:23-26; 18:15-22
Sharing the gospel	Matt. 28:19,20
Use clean language	Deut. 5:11; Matt. 5:33-37

Respect for people	Deut. 5:16; Rom. 13:7
Live with integrity	Deut. 5:18-20; Prov. 19:22; Acts 24:16
Live simply	Deut. 5:21; Matt 6:19-21; Mark 10:17-23
Equality in Christ	1 Cor. 12:12-30; Eph. 4:11-16; Jas. 2:1-10
Sanctity of all life	Deut. 5:17; Isa. 43:1-7; Luke 15:11-32; Eph. 2:4,5; Titus 3:4-7
Obedience to God's Word	Eph. 6:7,8; 2 Tim. 4:8; Jas. 1:12,25; 1 Pet. 5:1-4; Rev. 2:10
Community	Acts 2:42-47; 1 Cor. 12; Eph. 4:11-16
Servanthood	1 Cor 4:1; Eph. 2:10; Titus 3:8; Jas. 2:17; Rev. 22:12
Humility	Job 22:29; Prov. 3:34; 11:2; Matt. 5:3; Jas. 4:7-10
Sexual purity	Deut. 5:18; Matt. 5:27-30; Rom. 1:26,27
Excellence	Col. 3:23; 2 Tim. 2:15
Diligence	Dan. 12:12; 1 Cor. 9:24-27; 15:58; Gal. 6:7-10; Eph. 6:18
Cultural relevance	1 Cor. 9:19-22

The list of possible values is lengthy, of course. Others that could be added include discipline, freedom, honesty, family, commitment, godliness, righteousness, truth, justice, sacrifice, generosity, compassion, patience and faithfulness.

By taking the qualities listed in the Ten Commandments, the Beatitudes, the fruit of the Spirit and Paul's leadership standards (see 1 Tim. 3—4), you can create an impressive list of values to consider.

Don't accept them all, however, because the purpose of this exercise is to identify your *core* values—those that are absolutely central to shaping your character. No one would dispute the worthiness of any of the elements found in such passages of Scripture. When it comes to choosing those that are at the heart of your character, however, you must be more selective. Composing a laundry list of good qualities defeats the purpose of focusing on values.

You may choose to refine your list or perhaps expand it based upon experiences, emotions or intuition. The end result, regardless of the process, must be fully consistent with biblical truths and principles. If you supplement your values through extrabiblical means, be sure to refer to Scripture and verify that it corresponds to the qualities Christians are encouraged to possess.

As with the discernment of God's vision, your identification of, and commitment to, values should be accompanied by intense prayer. Values should not be a passing concern. They are the explication of who you are, and they represent part of your obligation to

God. You cannot take this lightly!

Before you initiate your values identification process, pray for God's wisdom and guidance. When you are in the midst of your reflections and decision making about values, pray for the Holy Spirit to direct your thoughts. After you believe you have arrived at a conclusive understanding of the values, seek His approval through intense prayer. Be open to God's Spirit challenging you about some of

> TAKE AWAY MY INTEGRITY AND I HAVE LITTLE TO OFFER AS A REPRESENTATIVE OF CHRIST, AS AN ANALYST OF THE AMERICAN CULTURE, AS A FATHER OF TWO YOUNG CHILDREN AND AS A LEADER IN A LOCAL CHURCH.

your proposed values.

Remember, you are identifying these values as a means of becoming a holy and pleasing sacrifice to Him (see Rom. 12:1) and so that you will be a capable visionary. The conclusions you draw about values are as important to God as they will be to you.

Your Core Values

It is helpful to realize that you may have various levels of values. I am primarily concerned with developing your core values. They are central in defining who you are. To breach a core value is to undermine your character, to detract from the essence of who you are and to violate your heart. Vision stems from your core values, not your secondary values.

Let's take an example. Two of my values are that I will live with integrity, regardless of the cost, and that I will live in Southern California, as God permits.

The first one is a core value for me: To defile my integrity would be to undermine who I am and to negate my sense of purpose in living. Take away my integrity and I have little to offer as a representative of Christ, as an analyst of the American culture, as a father of two young children and as a leader in a local church. The way I implement the vision for my life is intertwined with my ability to live with absolute integrity.

Consequently, when I have been offered opportunities, some of which fit within the vision for my life but conflict with my values, I have been able to make reasonable, consistent and defensible decisions.

For example, I have been asked to "ghostwrite" books for other people. In some cases, the books were based on data I had collected through our national research and were about topics that are dear to my heart. Writing those books would provide for me the opportunity to positively influence people's lives with truths that could transform their thinking and behavior for God's glory. But I also believe ghostwriting is unethical. Yes, it is a common practice, but that does not make it right, at least not in my code of ethics.

A matter of integrity. Thus, in spite of all the good reasons for ghostwriting books for some of the respected teachers and speakers in the Church today, my determination to maintain my integrity caused me to reject those tempting offers.

Objectively speaking, if I were to put all the reasons for writing those books on one side of the scale and place my desire to be a person of integrity on the other side, the balance would fall heavily in favor of writing such books.

Values, however, are not objective. They are the subjective content of who I am. Caving in to the temptation, even for such a potentially worthwhile and otherwise esteemable purpose, would make a mockery of my integrity. Exploiting those offers would compromise God's faith in me as a trusted servant and it would deny Him of the pride and pleasure due to Him through my life. Why? Because ghostwriting would undermine one of my core values.

If, for some reason, however, I had to move from Southern California and return to my childhood stamping grounds in the Northeast, I would pout and whine, but my character would not be undermined. The pleasant year-round climate of Ventura County, the proximity to the Pacific Ocean, the beauty of the landscape, the variety of recreational activities, all of these conditions germane to Southern California bring me great joy and peace.

Personal preference. Moving to a colder, more traditional and formal area of the nation would not redefine who I am. I could easily accomplish my vision for life from the Northeast, the South, the Midwest or the West: Location, in my life, is a matter of personal preference, not a matter of self-definition. Thus, living in Southern California is a secondary value. Even if it is compromised, my character is not.

As you reflect on your values be sure to distinguish between those that are core values and those that are secondary.

Value Statements

In providing examples of core values taken from other individuals and ministries, please realize that their values are not necessarily your values. You may examine these and relate to some, but not others. That does not mean these sources have improperly defined their values; nor does it mean you have incorrectly identified yours.

We are all different by God's design. Your values should reflect who you are and how God created you as a distinctive person. Similarly, your church is unlike any other, so its values are likely to be parallel but distinct from those of other churches although their missions are identical.

The following are a few values statements drawn from churches, parachurch ministries and Christian individuals.

Core Values of Willow Creek Community Church[2]

• Anointed teaching is the primary catalyst for transformation in the lives of individuals and in the church.

• Lost people matter to God, and therefore ought to matter to us.

• The church should be culturally relevant while remaining doctrinally pure.

• Christ's followers should manifest authenticity and yearn for continuous growth.

• The church should operate as a unified community of servants stewarding their spiritual gifts.

• Loving relationships should permeate every aspect of church life.

• Life change happens best in small groups.

• Excellence honors God and inspires greatness.

• Churches should be led by those with leadership gifts.

• Full devotion to Christ and His cause is normal for every believer.

Core Values of Glendale Community Church

These are the core values which we will strive to maintain in all communication, thoughts and activities undertaken as followers of Jesus Christ. These attributes display our heart for all to see; they represent the character we wish to possess; they stand as the criteria by which we will examine ourselves. All ministry endeavors emanating from our church should be consistent with these values:

• respect	• integrity
• faith	• joy
• forgiveness	• servanthood
• wisdom	• patience
• humility	• peace
• truth	• commitment
• love	• generosity
• righteousness	

Core Values of Eastside Foursquare Church

We value:

• an environment characterized by love, acceptance and forgiveness.

• the right of every person to choose for him/herself, and to make up his/her own mind on issues related to their personal life. This is a nondirective approach to Christian leadership.

• the serious approach to leadership in the management of our resources to the highest good of God's kingdom.

• a strong personal home life. We contend that local congregational life should be enhancing rather than destructive to the strength of the home.

• accountability. Our relationship with the Foursquare denomination is non-negotiable. The systems of accountability within and outside the Church are valued very highly and are considered essential to the maintenance of all for which we stand as the Church.

• holiness. We value our right standing before God, through Christ, as being righteous, without sin; and we contend for a life free of willful sin and disobedience to Christ.

• each other's personal relationship with Jesus Christ.

• the spontaneity of the Holy Spirit, the free expression of His gifts. We are committed to a serendipitous approach to the walk of the Holy Spirit, always being aware of the possibility of His intervention.

• the concept of the Church as a Force—the Church being Christ's heart, hands and mouth in our community.

• the liberty to express our unique, God-given call to our community as a congregation; the right to be who we are as a congregation, without regard to what has been or what is presently being done in other congregations or groups with reference to their approach to Christianity.

• the right of the Bible to interpret us.

• the historical roots of Christianity that have shaped the theology and orthodoxy of the faith.

Core Values of Focus on the Family[3]

• The Bible is our standard for all belief, instruction, practice and policy.

• We cannot do our work without a staff committed to Jesus Christ as Savior and Lord.

• We sincerely believe that prayer makes a critical difference in all that we attempt.

• We express our faith with a balance of head and heart, intellect and emotion.

• Our biblical principles and beliefs are not for sale, nor are they dependent on affirmation or acceptance by the culture.

• We will spare no effort to be reliable and accurate.

• We are determined to be fresh and creative in all of the various media we enter.

• Character is more important than talent.

• We invest every effort to avoid harming the cause of Christ.

• Power is dangerous. Our leaders must be careful not to abuse those they lead and must have strong accountability.

• We recognize and encourage God-given gifts in women as well as men, in members of all races and ethnic groups.

• We require that our senior leaders exemplify a history of personal faithfulness to their marriage vows from the point of conversion on.

• We listen carefully. Each constituent has something to teach us.

• We respond promptly and courteously.

• We are called to give generously to constituents as well as to receive their support.

• We pay special attention to the downtrodden, the poor, the discouraged, the oppressed, and those raising children alone.

• We treat one another with respect, as fellow laborers for God.

• We admit our fallibilities, promote collegiality and welcome a sense of humor in the workplace.

• We respect the various Christian traditions and loyalties of our co-workers.

• We intentionally focus more on meeting people's needs than on preserving or growing our institution.

• We identify as deeply as possible with people's hurts and concerns.

• We avoid self-congratulation.

• We pay close attention to detail at all levels, to offer Christ our best work.

• We create programs and services that are excellent without being ostentatious, attractive without being sensational.

• We are ancillary to the local church, and never intentionally compete for the church's people or funds.

• We are only one specialty within the Body of Christ. We enjoy spotlighting other worthy ministries that share our spiritual commitment.

Core Values of Charlie Hedges[4]

• Grace: treasure life as a gift from God; practice daily the privilege of loving God; be grateful and express gratitude.

• Human dignity: respect the rights and beliefs of others; seek first to understand before passing judgment; reject prejudicial talk and action; defend those who are absent; speak to people as they are, not as I wish them to be.

• Love: succeed at home first; embrace people with openness and acceptance.

• Hope: contribute to the felt self-value of others through word and deed; facilitate the growth and success of others; seek first to serve before being served.

• Integrity: always be real; acquire enough wisdom to be humble.

• Commitment and consistency: be diligent in small things in preparation for success in big things; never allow personal greed to interfere with loyalty.

• Growth and change: be willing to change, to learn and to grow.

• Fun: remember to find joy in my labor, for it too is a gift from God; have at least one hearty laugh each day.

• Value: do all things with quality.

• Impact: work to make a difference; grasp a vision for success; practice the courage to take risks.

Core Values of George Barna

• Glorify Christ: I exist to know, love and serve Jesus Christ. Everything I do must please Him and bring honor to Him.

• Experience success: success is radical obedience to God's vision for me and His commands for righteous living.

• Love my family: spend time with, love and encourage my wife and daughters to the best of my ability.

• Family spirituality: regularly invest time, effort and prayer in the spiritual development of my family.

• Integrity: demonstrating honesty, sincerity, respect, biblical morality and humility must be evident in all walks of my life; compromised integrity is failure.

• Service: receive and offer ministry.

• Self-acceptance: God loves me; therefore, I must love myself.

• Truth: the Bible is the source of absolute moral truth; it is my guidebook that defines the principles and standards by which I should live.

• Work: Barna Research is a means of serving God; I will respect employees, clients and suppliers, producing excellent products at fair prices.

• Stewardship: the resources I have—time, money, health, relationships, opportunities, reputation—should be used responsibly, for the benefit of my family, the Church and people in need.

• Personal growth: continual and intentional spiritual, intellectual and emotional growth is imperative.

- Acceptance: God, alone, is Judge; I am called to love, accept and forgive others.
- Renewal: regularly spend reasonable resources on moral and uplifting diversions to become emotionally, physically, spiritually and intellectually refreshed and to enjoy life.

In Conclusion

It should be clear by now that although all Christians, churches and parachurch ministries serve the same God and base their values and efforts on the same Bible, the values they cling to as their fundamental personal qualities vary.

So, too, does the way those values are expressed. There is no right or wrong way to communicate your values, and there certainly is no magic number of values to claim as your own. What is important is that the values you select are the right values for you, and that you live by them.

A Personal Challenge

If you have never written out your values, I encourage you to do so right now. This exercise is a means to a righteous objective. When you have identified those values, give them to a handful of trusted friends or family members and ask them to hold you accountable to those values.

Further, consider how your values relate to the vision you believe God has entrusted to you for your life. Take whatever steps are necessary to ensure that you are living consistently with your core values.

Check Your Church's Values

Consider your church. What are the core values it espouses? If you do not know, find out. Those values reflect the desired character of that Body. When you discover the core values, evaluate how well they correspond to what you believe the Church is to be and to how the ministry of your church is being implemented.

Again, consider the consistency of the church's mission, vision and values. Where inconsistencies appear to exist, discuss those concerns with leaders in the church.

Where opportunities exist for you to match your life vision with the vision and values of your congregation, get involved. Ministry is not a spectator sport. It is the lifeblood of a true Christian. Armed with a deeper understanding of what makes you and your church tick, you will be better able to serve with integrity, enthusiasm, energy, purpose and direction.

Notes

1. Hunter Lewis, *A Question of Values* (San Francisco: HarperCollins, 1990). Chapter 2 identifies the six ways, then Chapters 3 through 8 are devoted to describing each of the six ways in greater detail.
2. Lynne and Bill Hybels, *Rediscovering the Church* (Grand Rapids: HarperCollins/Zondervan, 1995), pp. 183-194.
3. "Our Faith, Values, Vision and Guiding Principles," *Focus on the Family* (Colorado Springs: 1995), pp. 8-11. Because of the length of the Focus statement, I have abbreviated the descriptions of a few of its values. If you wish to receive a copy of the entire booklet that describes the statement of faith, mission, vision and values, write to Focus on the Family, Colorado Springs, CO 80995.
4. Charles Hedges, *Getting the Right Things Right* (Sisters, Oreg.: Questar Publications, 1996).

The Mind of a Visionary

"THE CHALLENGES ARE NOT IN THE
MARKETPLACE. THEY ARE IN THE MIND."
—JEAN BENARD

I love to play basketball. That is not to say I am any good at it. If I had to feed my family based on my hoop skills, the four of us would be rail thin. Nevertheless, I enjoy the game and know that I have to pass the ball to a teammate who is not closely guarded if we are to score. My problem is one of timing. Usually, when I notice an open teammate our opponents have too, and they quickly move to defend my teammate and eliminate our scoring opportunity.

Pick-up basketball games generally are competitive because most amateur players are like me: They respond to circumstances as they occur. Rather than anticipate what is to occur, we wait for it to happen, then try to make the most of the moment.

Larry Bird, a superstar pro-basketball player in the 1980s, is hailed by many people as the greatest athlete ever to play the game. He was slow, couldn't jump high and suffered from a number of painful and limiting injuries to an elbow, knees and back. In spite of his limitations, however, he played at a level beyond others who were more physically gifted. Bird anticipated how the game would unfold. Players of my caliber move to where the ball is, in contrast to Bird, who would move to where the ball should be.

While watching the Celtics play, I often observed Bird at work. Rather than move to the spot where a player might be expected to go, Bird would move to maximize the opportunity. Bird, for example, might pass the ball to the spot where his teammate should be. On occasion, the ball would surprise the unsuspecting teammate, perhaps hitting him on the head, or even flying out of bounds, all because the teammate had not been thinking ahead and acting strategically.

A major difference between Larry Bird and me, other than the size of our respective bank accounts, is that I see things on the court as they are and try to make the most of what exists. I settle for what I see. Bird saw things that did not yet exist but would, partly because of his creative input, which enabled him to exploit what was about to happen. In his mind, the play had taken place. His actions merely followed through on what he had foreseen.

I play in the present moment; Larry Bird played in the future. He was like other great athletes who engage in team sports. Magic Johnson, Wayne Gretzky, Jerry Rice and other fabled athletes play the game slightly ahead of real time.

That is exactly how real-life visionaries think, too. Like Larry Bird, they see the future unfold in their minds, then act in strategic ways to facilitate that superior future. It is the ability—in most cases a learned, rather than purely natural ability—to think strategically and intentionally about the future.

Burt Nanus identifies the importance of such a style of thinking. "Indeed, vision is where tomorrow begins for it expresses what you and others who share the vision will be working hard to create. Since most people don't take the time to think systematically about the future, those who do—and who base their strategies and actions on those visions—have inordinate power to shape the future. Why else would such great historical figures as Moses, Plato, Jesus and Karl Marx have had such enormous influence on succeeding generations?"[1]

The Vision Process

I have discovered a progression in how people develop from visionless to vision driven. The visionless people view all change as a threat. They live in denial of the future, wedded to the past and the present, longingly remembering the way things used to be. Life is an endurance test for these folks, and frankly, hanging around them is a test of patience as well, especially for the vision driven. The visionless person lives by the motto: "It's all downhill from here."

The next step in the progression is to become open to consider the possibility that vision may be a stepping-stone to a better tomorrow. The people who reach this level live by a different motto: "Change is a necessary evil." Slowly and reluctantly, these people come to grips with the inevitability and the positive value of change.

The vision-seeking person is one who has finally embraced the true utility and hope represented by God's vision for the days to come. Having launched the journey to discover the vision God has for them, they are still insecure about their roles in this process and are still uncertain about the vision itself. They have turned the corner on the concept of vision, however, and are now actively pursuing the big picture. Perhaps the common motto of people at this stage of development is "There must be more to life than this."

At the pinnacle are the vision driven. Their entire lives are wrapped around the exhilarating potential released by the acceptance of God's vision for their lives and ministries. These people are oblivious to the debilitating analyses of a deteriorating society, because personally they no longer are part of the problem, but are part of the solution. Their motto: "The best is yet to come."

105

As in most walks of life, the transition from visionless to vision driven is a logical progression. For some people, the progression is quick and smooth; for others, it is difficult and prolonged. Some people make the transition based on observing reality or perhaps other visionaries.

Others make the transition by being mentored through personal attention, by reading and by intense communication with God. Such a transition appears to have no "average" means or schedule. The good news is simply that people do change as God wills. Any person who knows, loves and wants to serve God can become a visionary Christian.

Five Perspectives

Research illustrates the contrast between the thinking of visionary people and those who muddle through life. Those similarities and differences can be drawn in terms of five general perspectives: (1) how people perceive themselves, (2) the emotional input involved in decision making, (3) thought patterns, (4) perceptions about change and (5) responses to opportunities and obstacles.

1. Self-Perceptions

One of the most impressive qualities of visionaries is that they are always seeking to learn. No matter how significant their past accomplishments or how heralded their expertise, they invariably strive to absorb new truths, new principles, new data and new insights.

Visionaries are the kind of people the Bible refers to as wise. They have not yet decided what reality is, but recognize that it takes a busy, inquisitive mind to keep up with the ever-changing reality.

THE VISIONARY IS NOT INTERESTED IN WHO GETS CREDIT OR WHO ACTUALLY DOES THE WORK SO MUCH AS IN THE VISION BLOSSOMING AND PRODUCING FRUIT.

Nonvisionary people, on the other hand, have different goals: to become experts. Their views are that anyone who is not an expert has no business trying to dictate the terms of reality. The difficulty inherent in this perspective is that as soon as you master today's conditions, they are irrelevant because they are outdated. The only way to become an expert is to be a step or two ahead of the change curve.

Telephone-directory thinkers. People who live without vision are analogous to a telephone directory. The first day the new directory is printed, it is months out of date because of the time required to collect information, to check it, to prepare it for printing, to print it, to bind it and to deliver it. On day one of that process, the information generated for the directory was accurate and reliable; by the time the process had run its course, 10 to 15 percent of the numbers have changed (e.g., disconnected, changed to a new number) and another 10 percent of the existing numbers are missing. Visionary thinking precludes absolute accuracy in favor of perpetual discovery and anticipation.

A thoughtful difference. Visionary thinking also is translated into action differently from what the average person might assume. To nonvisionaries, personal responsibility requires that you roll up your sleeves and do the work of creating the better tomorrow. Therein lies one of the disincentives for many people to engage in visionary thinking. Nonvisionaries believe they are personally responsible for bringing vision to fruition. The concepts of teamwork, delegation and shared ownership are outside the realm of a vision-based reality in the minds of most people.

Facilitator or mechanic? The visionary thinker, however, takes a different approach. The visionary is not interested in who gets credit or who does the work so much as in the vision blossoming and producing fruit. Thus, the visionary thinker is a facilitator rather than a mechanic. This does not mean visionary thinking prevents a person from getting involved in the details and the grunt work that must occur for a vision to become a reality. It does, however, mean that visionaries are wise enough to recognize that most visions require more horsepower than they, alone, can muster.

The vision is not usually meant as a solitary order, but as a vision that must be communicated and jointly owned, then implemented by a team of like-minded people.

2. Emotional Response

Change is frightening for most people. It represents a journey into the unknown. People who have not developed a notion of why the future will be superior to the past and present, along with a sense of how to create that better future, have ample reason to be wary of the days to come. Their mental state leaves them powerless, helpless, sometimes even hopeless.

Faith replaces fear. Visionary thinkers refuse to succumb to such victimization. A visionary takes a proactive, rather than a reactive, approach to the future. Christian visionaries have sufficient faith in the promises of God to believe that He will provide the vision of a better tomorrow and the means to reaching that vision.

Such people avoid the emotional paralysis that fear of the future brings by taking personal responsibility for one piece of that future and by trusting that God will provide other believers who hold complementary pieces of a better future.

Most people look at reality and see the hardships and obstacles. Life is a series of challenges, fraught with pain and jeopardy. The typical American looks upon times of suffering as a negative period, a set of experiences to be avoided at all costs.

Hard times are no hindrance. Visionaries, in contrast, recognize that growth is difficult, sometimes painful. Without some degree of suffering, growth is not likely. Rather than design a comfortable future, visionaries work through the difficult times in the belief that such suffering is a means to personal maturity and is inevitable in breaking through to new heights of positive experience.

The vision-driven person realizes that pain and suffering are invaluable elements in the development process. Such hardships should be expected challenges in the path to growth. The visionary accepts such trials as a natural part of the journey to the desired objective.

This perspective on the inevitable—indeed, about the value of

107

hardships—enables the visionary to make different choices in daily activities. Although the person operating without vision sees the menu of alternatives and is likely to choose those that afford imme-

> THE VISIONARY THINKER JUSTIFIES THE RISK, REALIZING THAT IF NO RISKS ARE TAKEN, NO CHANGES WILL BE FORTHCOMING AND THAT THE ABSENCE OF CHANGE REPRESENTS A SETBACK, NOT PROGRESS.

diate comfort and security, the visionary is more likely to anticipate the future and to make choices that are risk laden.

The risks are justified. The visionary thinker justifies the risks, realizing that if no risks are taken, no change will be forthcoming and that the absence of change represents a setback, not progress.

Overall, visionary thinkers look upon safe choices as failure. The most significant breakthroughs in the human experience have been achieved at a cost. The sports axiom "no pain, no gain" is relevant to more than athletic contests. It is an axiom pertinent to life itself.

Visionaries make sense of the possibilities of hardship through mental and emotional filters that enable them to evaluate potential strife because of the ultimate benefits to be realized from such difficulty.

Nobody likes to endure pain and suffering, but the visionary thinker realizes that if growth requires such hardship, being able to anticipate the ultimate benefit of such discomfort produces purposeful endurance.

3. Thought Patterns

In speaking with visionaries, it has been fascinating to discuss how they arrived at their vision. The process is inevitably a long-term mixture of elements, such as prayer, Bible study, analyzing information about needs and opportunities in their life context, seeking verbal input from trusted colleagues, self-analysis and small-scale testing of elements of their developing vision. The way they organize their thoughts and deploy such components of evaluation is significant.

Most people live for the moment and think about their present experiences. Often they are focused on linking the present to the past as a means of making sense of their lives, of providing some knowable context for their deliberations.

A different point in time. Visionaries start at a different time point. They think as far into the future as their minds will allow, then work their way back to the present, force fitting the existence of their envisioned future into a possible path of development.

I find that visionaries learn to think creatively by abandoning the learned, cultural inclination to think in linear, sequential fashion in favor of a free-form, eclectic style. Visionaries, even those who are rigid and intellectual in their day-to-day operational mode, unleash their intuition, which has been prepared for such a creative adventure by the previous exposure to such things as data, prayer, Scripture and advice.

As visionaries focus on the future, they synthesize all that information into a manageable perspective on the future. The product is a new form of reality that will take serious retooling to move from the present to the desirable future.

Taming of the mind. Why don't most people practice unrestricted thinking? After all, wouldn't it be fun to let your mind go wild, unfettered by social conventions and personal limitations, mentally experimenting with new combinations and imagining unusual outcomes that would enhance humankind?

The answer is that most people are too scared by the unknown to pursue anything short of the predictable, even in their moments of wildest imagination. This helps us understand that becoming a visionary is a learned process that is made possible by the way God designed the human being. We have the mental and emotional capacity. The challenge is to release that capacity and to trust that God will use our natural talents, worldly experiences and hearts for service to arrive at practical and laudable conclusions. In short, we must trust God to allow us to think in revolutionary ways just as Jesus, Josiah, Paul and the rest of His servants did.

Faith acts as a centerpiece. Visionaries arrive at that point of trust through faith, which is at the center of godly vision. It also takes a willingness to look beyond process to product. If all you ever focus on is the means to the end, without investing your best thinking in the end, you are likely to develop the world's best process for a mediocre product.

The path followed by visionaries teaches us one more crucial element related to the nature of the result. True vision simplifies complexity. This is precisely why vision appeals to most people. It organizes a turbulent, ever-changing, sophisticated life system and makes it understandable and user friendly.

Americans struggle with life because they believe that success requires sophistication and complexity. In truth, progress demands the opposite: simplifying an already complex existence so that everyone can own a stake in creating a more livable, desirable and significant lifestyle.

4. Perceptions About Change

One of the major reasons most people resist change is that they believe it will introduce conflict into their lives. They look upon new strategies, new lifestyles, new perspectives as complications.

Visionary thinkers handle change differently. To them, change represents the natural progression of life. They look for the connections between what was, what is and what will be. In other words, they focus on continuity. In virtually every experience and circumstance in life, if we seek the connection point, we can find it. There are very few times when the future is totally unrelated to the past and present.

Agents of reconciliation. People who have no vision resist change. People who have vision embrace it as the necessary means of reconciling the known and the unknown. This perspective removes the anxiety that naturally occurs when considering the future. As visionaries, then, we are agents of reconciliation.

This stance is made possible because visionaries take the big picture into their ruminations. People who have no vision simply think small. They focus on the micro-environment and the details. Visionaries major on the macro-environment, believing that if God instills within them a vision for the future, He will provide whatever is necessary for the details to be accomplished.

Details are important in creating a better future, but true visionaries do not let the details deter them from owning the vision God has instilled in them. What is foolishness to humans may well be appropriate to God. Our finite minds are often too limited to understand the entire scope of what He has in store for us. As we place our trust in Him, and truly strive to absorb His vision for us, change is converted from a daunting, uncomfortable possibility to an exciting, high-potential probability.

5. Responses to Opportunities and Obstacles

Church leaders often encounter the incredulous response of nonvisionaries: "We can't do that. Do you know how much that would cost?" or "We don't have the people to take that on" or "That's just too much work." Visionaries, however, do not become discouraged by the small thinking of others. In response to challenges from people or circumstances, vision-driven individuals outthink the obstacles.

Visionaries work smart. In a prior job, I once heard my boss criticize a colleague for his lack of creativity in problem solving. "You work very hard, but you don't work very smart" was how she evaluated my colleague's efforts. That sums up how the visionary operates: working smart, rather than merely working hard.

Visionaries are never willing to shelve God's vision simply because the resources appear to be unavailable. I have learned that if the vision is from God, the resources will become available when necessary. Remember the needs of Nehemiah, and how the dearth of resources came from myriad unexpected places. One of the most remarkable truths about vision is that when the vision is implemented, the result is creating, rather than consuming resources.

Managers fill in details. Visionaries also refuse to be limited by the lack of detailed plans for making vision reality. Research has shown a big difference between a leader and a manager. In our present context, the leader is the person who conceives, through the hand of God, a vision for the future. Often a manager is then needed to work with the visionary to develop a plan for action in which all the details are thought through and the steps toward completion are systematically identified and followed.[2]

Because a visionary is a person who believes in the future, obstacles are viewed as opportunities. The visionary thinker truly embraces the words of the apostle Paul: "If God is for us, who can be against us?" (Rom. 8:31).

Notes

1. Burt Nanus, *Visionary Leadership* (San Francisco: Jossey-Bass Publishers, 1992), p. 8.
2. The distinction between a leader and a manager is discussed in a video presentation that is part of the video series entitled *The Church in a Changing Culture*, by George Barna, produced by Word Ministry Resources, Dallas, Texas, 1994. A related description is provided in a book about leadership, edited by George Barna, scheduled for publication by Regal Books in 1997.

The Life of a Visionary Believer

"IF A MAN HASN'T DISCOVERED SOMETHING HE
WILL DIE FOR, HE ISN'T FIT TO LIVE."
—MARTIN LUTHER KING JR.

The Profile of a Visionary

One of the greatest blessings in my life has been to know visionaries. Les Ingram is one of them. He has spent his life pouring his heart into serving the poor, including Native Americans and unreached Mexican people.

During the past half century of ministry, Les has encountered incredible obstacles and has endured significant frustrations while attempting to be a loving servant obeying God's call. His focus is never on the problems, only on the victories, the solutions and the possibilities.

Spending a day with Les is like a crash course in visionary behavior. He rises early to read his well-worn Bible and to pray. He allocates much of his time to those people he has been called to help. When Les talks with the poor on a reservation, they respond warmly. They sense his genuine interest in them and his determination to help them create a better environment.

Les devotes whatever time is necessary to create opportunities, to generate needed resources and to satisfy administrative requirements. Although he is a gifted person, he is wise enough to recognize his limitations and to rely on the assistance of others who have complementary gifts and abilities.

Focusing on Goals

Les succeeds where younger, more intelligent or more heavily financed people have failed for one reason: He always focuses on the goals that stem from his vision. Les is forever talking about the hurting people he meets and how he and his ministry partners can enhance their physical and spiritual lives.

Les communicates how simple, incremental acts of love can restore hope, dignity and purpose to the lives of the less fortunate. He motivates without manipulation by acquainting his partners with conditions and consequences and by encouraging them. As a result, he subtly empowers people to pursue positive change in the lives of others.

For many of us, time is a barrier to excellent performance. We do what we can in the time allotted. Les, however, does not worry about time. He does what it takes for however long it takes to meet the needs he has been called to address.

The simplicity of his lifestyle is merely a reflection of his finely tuned priorities and interests. A more complicated lifestyle would get in the way of his ministry imperatives. Like all visionaries I know, Les can seem absentminded, but he is anything but absentminded. More likely, he is mentally churning through scenarios and possibilities while the rest of us babble on about less significant matters.

Driven by Vision

When "Paco," as he is called, meets with impoverished or substance-abusing Native Americans, he addresses them with respect and compassion. His response is not always what you might expect, because it is filtered through the lenses of his vision. When he speaks to a Sunday School class, his fervor is not forced, but is irrepressible evidence of his compulsion to obey God's special calling.

He may be in his mid-70s, but Les maintains a sparkle and energy that shame men half his age. How does he do it? He is driven by the vision God has implanted in his mind. You cannot fail to be impressed by his will to serve, his commitment to God and the passion he has for seeing change occur in response to his faithful pursuit of vision. He serves strategically because he thinks strategically. He thinks strategically because he relates everything to his vision.

I pray that when I am in my 70s I will have the same single-mindedness of purpose, the same passion and the same inexhaustible energy that comes from full commitment to God's vision. Les has been an inspiration and a model to me. Like his fellow visionaries, I have learned a lot about God and about vision from his example.

Maybe you are not a Les Ingram, but do you exhibit the same single-mindedness of purpose, the same passion, the same inexhaustible energy because of your commitment to the vision God has for your life? If not, how badly do you want these qualities?

Visionary Living

The life of a visionary Christian is distinguished from that of the typical believer in four ways. Although such a comparison may appear strange, it is valid because fewer than 1 out of every 20 believers has discerned God's vision for his or her life and ministry. Visionary believers (1) behave differently, (2) they interact with other people differently, (3) they produce results differently and (4) they relate to God differently.

If you wish to evaluate not only the existence of God's vision in your life, but also the quality of your life as a visionary Christian, examine how you live today and contrast it to how you lived before you discerned God's vision for your life and ministry. To facilitate the comparison, rate yourself in relation to the following indicators:

1. Personal Behavior

Visionary Christians learn that the Bible is serious when it teaches us that time is precious. We have no clue when the end will come and when Jesus will return for His followers. We do know, however, until that moment arrives, we are being counted on by God to be His arms and legs, His hands and feet, His eyes, ears and mouth to a world that desperately needs His presence.

Visionary Christians use their time efficiently. Because they are aware of why they exist within His service, they can prioritize how they apply their resources. Because they have an understanding of the special function they are called to fulfill, they can view life with a laserlike focus.

Still have time for fun. They still have time for fun, they still experience frivolous moments and "down time," but visionary believers use different standards than other people in developing a daily schedule. Not surprisingly, then, these servants use God's vision as a conscious decision-making filter.

> ADVANTAGES ENJOYED BY CHRISTIAN VISIONARIES ARE THEIR ABILITIES TO MAKE TOUGH DECISIONS AND TO WEATHER THE CONSEQUENCES OF THOSE CHOICES.

If my observations are correct, it seems that visionaries can choose from a greater pool of wonderful opportunities. For those people who lose their focus and begin to make choices without reference to their vision, this plethora of opportunities can easily paralyze, or at least neutralize, their effectiveness for Christ. The visionaries who continue down the straight and narrow path, however, experience the joy and fulfillment provided by such discipline and purposefulness. One measure of how satisfying this discipline is for visionaries is that they consistently examine each new opportunity by considering its relationship to their special calling.

Advantages enjoyed by Christian visionaries are their abilities to make tough decisions and to weather the consequences of those choices. In some instances, they contend with the emotional debris of having rejected appealing or prestigious opportunities for their lives and ministries because the options conflicted with the vision.

In other cases, visionaries are able to select the most appropriate option because the vision provides purpose and direction. Visionaries do not suffer from lasting disappointment about rejecting appealing alternatives. Because they have such a useful guide, they simply trust that God will take care of them in the best possible manner as long as they are faithful and obedient servants.

Vision builds courage and wisdom. Beyond rejecting appealing choices, visionaries benefit from their vision because it provides the courage and wisdom to make tough decisions. When visionaries make unpopular or personally difficult decisions and stick to those choices because of the vision, they invariably are stronger and are better positioned as a result.

The test of remaining true to the vision, regardless of the challenges, is part of the refining process that all visionaries experience. As you prove yourself to be capable and trustworthy, expect to find that God will provide other opportunities for service (see Matt. 25:21,23; Luke 16:10; 19:17,26).

Most parents, of course, learn this underlying principle early in their child-rearing period. After agonizing trials and tribulations, good parents tend to discover that setting limits often is the greatest gift they give their children. Establishing parameters and holding children accountable help them develop godly characters and convictions. Similarly, God's vision is one of His ways of helping us recognize the most profitable parameters for our lives and ministries.

Visionaries learn to persevere. Visionary Christians are distinctive in that they persevere, too. The basis of their diligence in the face of adversity is their conviction that they are on a track determined by God and that God will bless their determination to remain obedient.

Visionaries become accustomed to adversity, recognizing that as champions of one small but significant portion of the Lord's plan, they are enemies of Satan. Tribulations can thus be expected, as a declared enemy of the evil one. Christian visionaries, however, are well armed to handle the battle. All it takes is faith in Christ and commitment to His cause as portrayed through the mission and vision they possess.

Another key characteristic of vision-led Christians is that they are in the game for its duration. If your church is typical, you observe people whose commitment comes and goes, just as they do. But once you have God's vision, you are in too deep to turn back.

Remember, God only gives His vision to those people who are serious about a life of meaningful service. When you reach the point at which He has provided a vision for your life and ministry, you will have fully surrendered yourself to God and will have beseeched Him for a significant quest as a life commitment. At that point, you join a special cadre of believers, akin to the mythical Knights of the Round Table in King Arthur's Court. You are now a "career visionary." You are in it for the long haul.

Attitude about life and ministry is another behavioral characteristic common to Christian visionaries. Objectively speaking, the future offers little hope. Violence, pornography, broken families, substance abuse, poverty, life-curtailing diseases, natural disasters, international wars, illiteracy, racial animosity appear on the list of hardships and cultural deterioration.

Yet, vision-directed Christians maintain the most optimistic and hopeful perspectives about the future. They are, after all, involved in the spiritual redemption and interpersonal redevelopment of the world, employed by the Lord Jesus Christ. Their efforts are not wasted or senseless, but are purposeful and influential. They understand their investment in the vision to be a vital part of the solution to the complex problems of their world.

Combined with the pursuits of the millions of other vision-led believers across the globe, they reason, it is unthinkable that God would not bless their cumulative service. Yes, they are more enthusiastic about the future than the naked facts merit, but then, visionaries have foreseen a future the rest of the world has not even dreamed of.

2. Personal Interactions

If you are a vision-driven follower of Christ, you demonstrate your vision in your conversation. Visionaries talk about the heart of the vision. They describe it to others, they encourage others to join them in their vision quests, they express frequent gratitude for the directions they have been given in life, they relate news and public events to their causes.

In essence, visionaries are obsessed with their vision. To the non-visionary folk, visionaries may seem unidimensional or narrow-minded. Among fellow visionaries, however, especially those who share the vision, they are the most interesting and significant leaders in the world.

To those people who successfully enlist the involvement of other people in their campaigns to realize the vision, they become cheerleaders, encouraging and thanking colleagues for their participation. I have seen several introverted visionaries become much less relationally isolated because of their burning desires to transform their vision from one-person crusades into mass movements.

Human nature can change. I had a teacher in high school who preached that "human nature never changes." She was wrong; the power of the gospel can radically transform hearts, and the lives of believers can also be forever redefined by their complete commitment to Someone and to something bigger than themselves—God's vision.

Visionaries exude a sincere interest in another person's vision and expect to find the same level of intensity and exuberance in the lives of other believers as they do in their own. Visionaries eventually, and unconsciously, become inclined to view other people in reference to vision. If they encounter a fellow visionary, the relationship is likely to hinge on a mutual understanding of, appreciation for and desire to assist the other person in fulfilling a vision.

Because visionaries are focused, they often want to know how they can help the other person accomplish his or her vision, or at least understand how their respective visions can be compatible and mutually beneficial.

During the 1992 presidential campaign, members of the media delighted in labeling Bill Clinton and his vice presidential running mate, Al Gore, as "policy wonks." Journalists reported that the two men spent hours discussing the fine points of public policy, often following a draining, bruising day on the campaign trail.

Those conversations may well have been what recharged the candidates' physical and emotional batteries that sustained them throughout the campaign. Clinton and Gore were driven by a vision of using government as a means to create a better society. They spoke each other's language—the visionary language of liberal policy makers driven to help humanity through government intervention and assistance.

A feeling of family. Most Christian visionaries are either part of the vision-savvy family or are nice people who have yet to mature fully. Often the visionary feels sad for the visionless believer, recognizing that the latter is missing out on one of the most meaningful elements of the Christian experience. It is similar to the heartbreak an evangelist feels for a non-Christian.

Because visionaries are driven to fulfill their appointed tasks, they tend to be unusually open to be partners with individuals or ministries that could enhance their own abilities to fulfill the vision. Instances in which attitudes hinder cooperation usually occur when the vision is not from God or when the visionary is struggling with an errant ego. Those who truly understand the calling, though, realize that God's vision is usually so substantial that it takes more than their own best efforts to accomplish the task. Gaining the support of other believers is welcomed.

Likewise, because vision-driven believers are serious about their special callings, they usually are eager to have others hold them accountable for implementing the vision. Accountability is not always a pleasant experience, of course, but most of the saints who seek to serve God accept the need to be evaluated by others who care about the Lord and about the visionary.

Learning from others. One of the most valuable attributes of vision-driven believers is the desire to learn from other people. Perhaps because vision is too big for us to accomplish on our own, visionaries invite the help of others. In a world loaded with information, relational networks, experts and other resources, the true servant of God wants nothing but the best for the Master and realizes that he or she does not have a perfect understanding of the ministry environment. Seeking the advice and wisdom of others can save scarce resources for use in promoting the vision.

3. Productivity

There are exceptions to every rule, and this one is no different. Yet, more often than not, I find that when God's visionaries make discernible progress toward their vision-related goals, they give the glory for their successes to God. This should not be considered unusual; every believer is called to give constant thanks and praise to God for the many blessings and miracles He provides for us every day.

> VISIONARY BELIEVERS ARE DISTINGUISHED BY THEIR PRAYER LIVES. THEY PRAY WITH GREATER FREQUENCY, GREATER FOCUS, GREATER URGENCY AND GREATER OPENNESS BECAUSE OF THEIR HUMILITY AS A RESULT OF THE VISION.

Yet, the truth is that most people—yes, even most believers—take for granted the many wonderful things that happen in their lives. To their credit, and probably because they are overwhelmed by the magnitude of their special purposes, visionaries are more likely to acknowledge that any success was God's doing, not their own. The scope of His expectations for us is one of the beauties of vision because it increases our dependence upon Him while He invests a greater degree of trust and confidence in us.

Visionaries accomplish great things for God because they focus on the vision, because He blesses their efforts and because visionaries engage in frequent and realistic evaluations of how they are faring in their vision quest.

Many are tempted to simply revel in the fact that they have been counted worthy to do specific functions in His grand plan for humanity, but ultimately they recognize that excellence in the performance of their duties on His behalf requires rigorous examination.

Living by strict standards. We serve a God who has imposed standards on people time after time. In doing His bidding, we need to reach reasonable standards to make the grade—not to earn His love, but simply to maximize our resources for the One we love and have the honor of serving. We will never gain righteousness in His eyes by the level of performance we reach, but a natural part of our growth as believers and servants is to seek to do our best with the resources provided to us.

Maybe the best way to put this is that visionaries work hard. They are driven, not by the applause or the baubles of the world, but by the chance to please God. Visionaries also work smart. They seek the optimal utilization of resources toward the speediest and most perfect outcomes. In other words, Christian visionaries are not mere plodders; they are strategic zealots.

4. Spirituality

I have observed all manner of delusion within the Christian community. Some people have replaced the heart of God with the statutes of God and have worshiped an empty form of our Father. Others have created divisiveness based on their interpretations of God's Word or on their style preferences—megalomania, idolatry, power and lust— you name it, and somewhere in the United States, under the banner of Christianity, it probably exists.

I mention this not to denigrate the Church, but to contextualize the realization that something as personal as vision could easily be abused. The "new age" churches espouse the importance of vision for life, but the vision they describe is from within, for self, and is not attached to any external base of accountability other than public law.

Steering clear of abuse. Fortunately, Christian visionaries are touched by the might and grandeur of God. It is their ability to sense His majesty and His abundant love, His indescribable power alongside His boundless compassion that steers them clear of abusing the concept of a special and unprovable vision that is given to every authentic follower of Christ.

For vision-led Christians, the vision is acknowledged as a gift from God, but despite the power of the vision, it never replaces God. It remains His instrument of direction for our resources after we voluntarily submit all we have to Him.

Visionary believers also are distinguished by their prayer lives. I find that they pray with greater frequency, with greater focus, with greater urgency and with greater openness because of their humility as a result of the vision. They ask for guidance, wisdom, blessing and resources. They pray with reverence. They know that without Him, His vision will go unfulfilled.

121

Indicators of Visionary Living

Personal Behavior:
1. Efficient use of time: ministry-driven priorities.
2. Vision is a conscious decision-making filter.
3. Willing to make the tough decisions on the basis of the vision.
4. Anticipate barriers and obstacles because of their commitments to the vision; not discouraged by challenges.
5. Prepared to be in ministry service, based on the vision, for the long haul.

6. Altered attitude: more hopeful and optimistic than circumstances merit.

Personal Interactions:
1. Strategically communicate the vision to others.
2. Enlist support of the vision from others.
3. Encourage those who labor with them in pursuit of the vision.
4. Intentionally thank those who colabor in the vision.
5. Open to partnering with any individuals or ministries that could enhance their ability to fulfill the vision.
6. Always seeking to learn from other people.
7. Willingly place themselves in accountability relationships.
8. Consider every relationship in terms of the other person's vision and how he or she might help the other person reach a vision.

Productivity:
1. When they achieve progress toward the vision, they give the glory to God.
2. Frequent and realistic evaluations of how they are faring in their vision quest; evaluation leads to excellence.
3. Operate strategically; work hard and smart.

Spirituality:
1. The vision is a gift from God, but it never replaces God.
2. Constant prayer for guidance, wisdom, blessing and resources.
3. Genuine worship, fueled by their awe at being used by Him, and by His faithfulness to their efforts.

The Practical Visionary

Visionary living is more than simply being able to focus on the vision you have received from God. Christian visionaries integrate the elements that make their vision practical. A true visionary believer is one who lives in harmony with his or her mission, vision, values, gifts and abilities.

Life is comprised of an unending string of opportunities and challenges that demand decisions. Average Americans are terrible decision makers. Why? Most of them have little understanding about why they exist or what they hope to accomplish. Lacking a clear understanding of mission, vision, values, gifts and abilities, people find that every decision is difficult, if not overwhelming, because no standard or useful framework exists for making sense of available options. When they have a precise understanding of life's purpose, decisions are easier to make by filtering facts through a consistent grid.

In the preceding chapter, I discussed the notion of developing an integrated life, making life-defining decisions and living in harmony with the mission, vision, values, gifts and abilities instilled by God.

The following examples show how people I know have addressed some of the challenges in their lives by using—or, unfortunately, by not using—the tools of an integrated life with vision as a necessary ingredient in the mix.

Vision Was Used as an Excuse

A man I'll call Gary approached life much as many other people do in the Body of Christ. He understands his mission, has worked through his values and has identified God's vision for his life. He has extraordinary creative gifts and abilities. Gary, however, is an inert Christian. He attends church services every weekend, faithfully gives money to his church and participates in a small group. Yet, he never participates in the ministries of the church or in a personal ministry.

123

I asked Gary why he doesn't contribute to the work of Christ, given his giftedness and the myriad opportunities he encounters in his life. This isn't the time, he responded. After an increasingly heated discussion, we parted, still friends, but with a clearly divergent view of what the Christian life is about.

A short time later, Gary was invited to be interviewed by a Sunday School teacher in the church about his experiences working in a secular industry where few Christians were present. No preparation would be needed. No "right" answers were expected of him.

Gary was a perfect candidate because he had been exposed to the tensions experienced by a person "being in the world and of the world," which the class was studying. Although Gary knew the people in the class, was friendly with the teacher, was not intimidated by appearing in public and had no other obligations during the time the class was scheduled to meet, he declined the invitation.

The teacher asked Gary a second time, describing how Gary would be helpful to the group. He declined again. Two members of the class called to implore Gary to help them in the class's struggle to understand the biblical concept in question. Again, Gary rejected the opportunity.

Why had Gary denied others the opportunity to learn from his experiences and reflections? "It's not what I'm about," he explained to me, which is his way of saying such an adventure did not fit within the boundaries of his vision. I pressed him. Wasn't such an opportunity consistent with his mission and his values and certainly represented a comfortable fit with his skills? Was the option to address the class inconvenient? No. Was it scary? No. Was it consistent with his mission and values? Yes. Was it inconsistent with his vision? No, just outside his definition of the vision.

Although Gary referred to his vision when making the decision, he was essentially using his vision as an excuse. Nothing was inconsistent about sharing his experiences with the class for 30 minutes.

Gary's decision was made because the strategies he had concocted did not include this particular alternative. Denying the opportunity based on his vision was spiritual laziness. He could have satisfied part of his mission ("to serve God and His people with authenticity") and remained true to his values (e.g., openness, excellence, diligence, honesty). I believe Gary's choice actually undermined his ability to live in harmony with his mission and values.

A CEO Decision

One of the largest employers in my area is a movie studio. It has earned a reputation for requiring incredible loyalty and hard work from its employees. Those in management know that the CEO is a hands-on person and devotes enormous hours to building the studio's kingdom. One of the dictums of the core group of leaders is that attendance at the weekly Sunday morning strategy session is mandatory. One participant informed me that the rule of thumb was: "If you don't make it Sunday morning, you might as well not get out of bed Monday morning."

A Promotion Offering Perks

Consider Walt's dilemma. He was offered a promotion at the studio, which would include a hefty salary raise and superior benefits. The added salary would ease the financial tension in his household, including braces for one daughter, the opportunity to move to a bigger home in a better neighborhood, the chance to move their children into private schools and his wife could leave her job and devote herself to being a full-time mother.

A spiritual benefit was included in the promotion. Walt, for example, would be the only Christian in the inner circle, which presented an opportunity for positive influence on this powerful group of executives.

Upward mobility, however, always comes with a price. Perhaps the most significant price for Walt was the Sunday morning meeting and the late hours expected every night. Church services would be out. Not only would he have to stop leading his Bible study group, which met Tuesday evenings, but he would also be unable to attend the group. Walt realized that the choice was a more comfortable lifestyle versus consistent spiritual commitment.

For Walt, this choice was agonizing but clear cut. His mission did not prevent him from considering the new position. His vision and values, however, which related to being the ever-maturing spiritual head of his family, putting God first in all things, valuing community and relationships more than materials and comfort and achieving balance in life, screamed, "NO!"

Walt knew that if he refused the promotion, he probably would never have a similar opportunity and that his current position might be jeopardized. His faith in God's provision and his determination to stand firmly by his mission, vision and values gave him the courage to decline the tempting offer.

The Peter Principle

Jack was the most popular teacher in the adult Sunday School program at his church. For several years, his classroom was packed with peers who were committed to his teaching. The class was the highlight of Jack's week, too. Gifted as a teacher, he enjoyed preparing for the weekly sessions and practically glowed when leading his class through the Bible and its applications. He was in his element.

This opportunity to use his gifts and abilities during the weekly forum was fully consistent with the vision for ministry God had given to Jack. One of the reasons Jack had stayed at that particular church was that it provided a platform to utilize his gifts.

Why Not Direct the Sunday School?
Then elders of the church, cognizant of Jack's stellar abilities in the Sunday School, offered him the directorship of the entire Sunday School program. He would have the opportunity to define the direction of the program and to recruit and train other teachers. Jack would also have the opportunity to evaluate the soundness of the program, be involved in the administrative decisions and address the other challenges emanating from any Christian education program at a growing, mid-size church.

To the elders, Jack seemed the only realistic choice. He was, after all, their best teacher, a strong advocate of Bible-based education and a respected member of the church. This would be the next step toward his probable future as an elder in the church.

When the word spread that Jack was in line for the prestigious position, many people congratulated him on his good fortune. They encouraged him to take the job because of his obvious love of teaching, his devotion to the adult education program and the church's need for a competent Sunday School director.

Jack Draws on Vision

Jack was not nearly as excited about the possibilities as were his peers. He was savvy enough to recognize that he was unintentionally being set up to become the next victim of the Peter Principle. This is the axiom popularized in the 1970s by Lawrence Peter that says a person will continue to be promoted until he or she reaches the level at which they are incompetent and therefore no longer deserve to be promoted. They are then either left to create confusion and chaos in that position or to be fired. Jack, however, was not reflecting on the offer because of the Peter Principle. He was mulling about the position in consideration of his gifts, abilities and vision.

Jack's gift was being a teacher, not an administrator. Becoming the director of the program would likely remove him from the classroom, would require that he concentrate on administration rather than lesson preparation and would refocus his attention from the personal spiritual growth of his students to the overall health of the educational program.

Jack's abilities had repeatedly shown that handling paperwork and sitting through meetings (much less organizing and chairing them) were not part of his makeup. He had a strong distaste for mediating conflict. Working with budgets was something he left to his wife. Elderhood was an honor, certainly, but it was not one he coveted. He was not willing to sacrifice the greatest joy in his life for this honor.

The clincher for Jack was his vision: "I will exploit all opportunities to expose adults to God's truth, to help them understand and apply those truths in creative ways to all walks of their life and to demonstrate God's truth and principles through my own life." As Jack reflected on how the directorship would facilitate fulfilling his vision, it became clear that it would block, rather than enhance, his call to being a purveyor of truth, understanding, application and example. He graciously declined the offer.

Jack's church had indicated that it needed him to assume the position. The elders had intimated that this was their final checkpoint in evaluating his fitness for a higher level of church leadership. Was it selfish for Jack to reject the position? Was it foolish? Was it shortsighted, resigning him to a classroom when he could have become a more influential force in the future of the congregation?

Who Is to Be Served?

The answer to all these questions is no. It would have been selfish for Jack to take the new post because the primary value that choice would serve was for his good, rather than for those whom he might serve. As for foolishness, it would be more absurd to consciously accept challenges he was neither designed to enjoy nor master, nor that excited nor motivated him. Becoming an elder is too important a position to accept simply because it is available for the taking.

I respect high-profile politicians who have declined the opportunity to seek the presidency because they believe the process would harm their family lives or because they believe they have the public popularity but not the requisite skills and gifts to adequately serve the nation.

Jack exhibited the same kind of wisdom, recognizing this "great opportunity" was great only for someone whose gift was leadership or administration, whose abilities included conflict resolution and organizational management and whose vision incorporated the key elements of directing a core ministry of a church.

Self-Doubt Turns to Victory

The last two stories have been about friends who turned to their vision and values as decision-making guides and have emerged with red light flashing. Let me tell you about another friend, Terry, who was inclined to reject an opportunity, but changed his mind after considering that option considering his vision, values, gifts and abilities.

Terry had served as a top-level executive for more than a dozen years in a major international evangelistic ministry. The essence of his vision was to use his gifts of evangelism and leadership to facilitate the spread of the gospel to other nations of the world. This was to be accomplished by developing significant interpersonal relationships among believers and nonbelievers, enabling the proclamation of the gospel and subsequent discipleship.

Tempting Offers Received

Intelligent and a hard worker, Terry had accomplished some amazing things during his tenure, but as changes took place in the ministry, he began to look elsewhere for employment.

Within a few months, Terry received offers from a variety of organizations. The offers were varied: president of an educational institution, director of a counseling ministry, associate pastor at a church, CEO of an evangelistic ministry to college students and developer of an overseas conference ministry.

Each offer had its strengths and weaknesses. The personal benefits were divergent: prestige, salary, emotional gratification, travel, speaking opportunities and so forth. The problem for Terry was not the absence of opportunities; it was an abundance of appealing alternatives.

Although Terry dutifully pursued several of the possibilities, the option that seemed most riveting was to become the CEO of an evangelistic group that works with young people from other nations.

Struggling Group Needed Help

The small organization was struggling and declining in size and influence, was in bad shape financially and the staff was in disarray. The pay was less than that available from the other positions, and as CEO Terry would have to quickly raise money to guarantee he would get paid at all. The ministry was located in an area of the country that was not especially appealing to him.

Terry's natural inclination was to look for something more stable and secure, especially because the needs of his family were on the line. Yet the position kept coming to mind. As he prayed and fasted about the choices available, he also considered how God had prepared him for service. He soon realized that his heartbeat—that is, his vision—was not focused upon achieving a comfortable, secure job, but upon developing significant evangelistic opportunities and systems. He recognized that his primary gifts would be wasted in educational institutions and counseling centers.

Terry's natural abilities, especially in terms of relationships and public speaking, were better suited to the struggling evangelistic enterprise than to the prestigious and stable entities competing for his attention. Perhaps part of the caution he felt was the fear of personal failure in such daunting circumstances.

Vision Met the Need

Ultimately, Terry chose to accept the CEO position. The deciding factor for him was the fit between the organization's vision and his own, the parallel between the values it embraced and those he lived and the organization's need for someone who had exactly the kinds of gifts, abilities and experiences he offered.

Yet, it was still a decision based on faith, a faith that God was leading Terry into that position to succeed, not to fail. Had Terry taken the job based on feelings and emotions, he would have taken the church position. Had he chosen on the basis of financial security or occupational prestige, he would be in the educational community today. For Terry, though, the clincher was vision and gifts.

If you want to be a true visionary, someone who is grateful for God investing His trust and His vision in you, don't treat the vision as if it were an optional resource that can be used or ignored according to your personal whims. Treat it as the incredible blessing it is, using the vision as a central decision-making, heart-checking element.

Do not simply possess God's vision for the sake of knowing the kind of future God wants you to help create; live as a visionary would!

The Life of a Visionary Church

"THOSE WHO SAY IT CANNOT BE DONE
SHOULD GET OUT OF THE WAY OF THOSE
WHO ARE DOING IT."
—ANONYMOUS

Finding a Church

A decade ago I lived in a town in the Midwest that was often thought of as the capital of American evangelicalism. My wife, Nancy, and I moved there from Los Angeles, where we had been intimately involved in a good church. Although we were wary of the heavy-duty winters we knew we would be facing in the Midwest, we were excited about being called to serve in a special ministry.

We also were looking forward to interacting with churches in the "evangelical capital." As relatively new Christians, we thought this would be a monumental step forward in experiencing the best of what the Church had to offer.

After making the big move and experiencing some serious winter snowfalls, my wife and I experienced the biggest letdown of our lives. We spent every Sunday and many Wednesday evenings during the first year visiting churches, striving to find one that met our need for active, vital spirituality.

A Life-Changing Experience

Instead, Nancy and I found tired, routine, humdrum Bodies that had good reputations. We tried our best to be open-minded and flexible in our expectations and needs. We could not help but conclude that these churches simply lacked the zeal, the passion, the energy we had excitedly anticipated. We were ready to give up, leave our jobs and return to California where we knew we could once again enjoy spiritual vitality within a church home.

Noting my brooding state and ascertaining that it was because of severe disappointment about the local church scene, one of my assistants suggested yet another church to investigate. The church was new to me and was located a considerable distance from our home. My associate's sales pitch wasn't too convincing either. She confided that she had stopped attending there more than a year ago and that it was not a "mainstream" church. In my desperate state, though, any possibility was viable. So I agreed to check it.

The following Sunday proved to be a turning point in my life. The church that had been suggested was Willow Creek Community Church, pastored by Bill Hybels. This was in the early 1980s, before Willow Creek became a 15,000-member congregation and a national church phenomenon. Willow Creek was unlike any church my wife and I had experienced, but it was exactly what we sought because it was a church that had a clear vision—a vision that aroused the passion of staff and members.

Some Churches Lacked Vision

In retrospect, I recognize that the problem with the other 13 churches we had explored was not that they were heretical or outdated. The problem was that they had no vision driving the ministry. Anything and everything was acceptable, change was unnecessary, ministry effect was a minor concern and few criteria for ministry evaluation were in place.

The notion of evaluating the ministry was outside the boundaries of these churches' thinking. They were full of good people, brothers and sisters in Christ who love Him, but who had unintentionally (and unknowingly) devolved into religious country clubs. They went through the motions every week and had the best of intentions, but they had become the modern-day equivalent of the lukewarm, ineffectual church in Laodicea, depicted so pointedly in Revelation 3.

What caused Nancy and me to excitedly make the long drive to Willow Creek two or three times each week and to become actively involved in its community and ministry endeavors was the focus and the passion that were so evident at that church.

We Became Die-Hard "Creekers"

Granted, Willow Creek's size and its style would not appeal to everyone. Neither would its vision. The church offered great preaching, but we had heard fine teaching elsewhere, too. No, the magnetic quality was the heartbeat of the church. It was the first time we had encountered a church that was so up front, so clear and so committed to the unique vision God had given to that body.

We became die-hard "Creekers" during our tenure in the Midwest because we were drawn by the fact that this was a church filled with people who were living as Christians should. For this group of saints, vision was not an ethereal concept; it was a way of life. On more than one occasion, Nancy and I remarked that we felt as if we had stumbled into Jerusalem in A.D. 33 and were experiencing the church of Acts 2. That exposure to vision-driven faith has forever changed my life and my ministry.

133

The Visionary Church

If the local church is to be a visionary ministry unit, it must possess the same characteristics as those found in a visionary individual, which were discussed in the previous chapter.

The activities of a visionary church are startlingly different from those of churches that seek to serve God without true vision. The choices include (1) what to do in ministry, (2) how to allocate resources, (3) the kinds of relationships to foster, (4) the frequency and methods used to evaluate church efforts and (5) the ways it integrates its spirituality with those activities.

Vision Enhances Efficiency

Churches that have a well-articulated and widely owned vision from God tend to be more efficient in their operations because of their focus. They make decisions that are sometimes unpopular, but they accept those choices without the usual congregational rancor as long as the decision is vision consistent.

These churches address the future with gusto and confidence

because they believe they are in the race until the end. Visionary churches are churches of hope, not only the hope that resides within us because of our salvation, but also the hope that the congregation will be used in astounding ways to influence the lives of more people, in more ways, than would ever have been imagined or possible without His vision for the church.

> VISION-BASED CHURCHES CONSIST OF VISION-LED PEOPLE. THESE CHURCHES HAVE VISIONARY LEADERS WHO ARTICULATE, CAST AND CHAMPION THE VISION ON BEHALF OF THEIR CHURCHES.

A Vision-Led People

Vision-based churches consist of vision-led people. These churches have visionary leaders who articulate, cast and champion the vision on behalf of their churches. These are churches in which the people converse about the state and progress of their vision quest and receive more than blank stares from those with whom they speak.

These are churches in which networking means more than distributing business cards for potential business relationships. It entails developing a web of associations in which each other's gifts and experiences are considered as a potential and available means to advancing a person's vision.

These are churches in which people still have their secrets—they are, after all, still fallible, sinful people—but they have an increasing involvement in mutual examination and accountability. These are churches in which the people have a heart to learn from the Bible, from their leaders, from each other and directly from God.

God Gets the Credit

When a visionary church reaches a milestone or achieves a small victory on the road to vision fulfillment, the recognition is given to God for His graciousness. Yes, the people involved are recognized for their roles, too, but these churches see vision as the ultimate partnership: their church with other churches, their people with other people and everyone with God. The worship, the prayers, the programs are developed to be consistent with the vision and to glorify God.

It is easy to ascertain whether a church is vision driven. Examine how the church handles significant change within its ministry context. The vision-driven church *creates* change. Consequently, it is well prepared to handle the consequences of transformation in the context. A visionless church *reacts* to change. As a result, it is usually the victim of unanticipated realities for which it is ill prepared.

Does this description of the visionary church paint too idyllic a portrait? If so, it may mean that you or your church have not yet matured in the vision-development process.

The challenge to this alluring characterization of visionary churches is valid, not because the portrait is contrived or erroneous, but because you may never have encountered a church in which God's vision is the centerpiece of the ministry or in which visionary Christians fill the pews.

Based on our nationwide research among Protestant churches, I estimate that less than 4 percent have an articulated vision statement that has been heard, understood, accepted and embraced by the congregation. Our national research among adults suggests that perhaps as little as 3 percent of all believers have truly determined God's vision for their lives. These are appallingly minuscule numbers!

Naturally, when a visionary church is found, the chance of having visionary believers in the pews is much higher if only because they have been exposed to and trained to consider vision.

135

Common Reactions to the Vision

Perhaps it would help to describe the four primary responses of church people to vision: (1) denial, (2) coexistence, (3) acceptance and (4) ownership. Think about your church, its current vision status and where the church seems headed in relation to God's vision for that ministry. Where does your church fit on this continuum?

Some Churches Are in Denial

The worst-case scenario is the church that is in *denial*. The people of these congregations are actively fighting the vision, dead set on rejecting it. Sometimes they are openly hostile to it. This response is most common among congregations that are inwardly focused and those that are dominated by people 60 or older. This response is also common among congregations that have been numerically flat or in decline for some years, those that are part of denominations that are experiencing decline and those in which the pastor has not sufficiently won the confidence of the people to play the role of visionary leader.

Vision does not find a toehold in those bodies, because the ultimate purpose of these congregations has little to do with ministry. They are focused on preservation and survival.

Some Churches Are Willing to Coexist

The next step up the continuum are congregations that are willing to *coexist*, albeit at arms length, with the vision. They will neither fight it nor support it. Their underlying hopes are that the vision will go

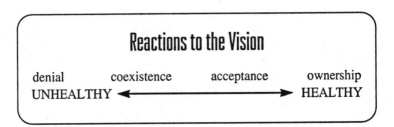

away. Some members hope the vision-development process is just the latest in the series of popular techniques pastors seem to explore.

In general, the people in these churches are apathetic about the vision and waste no energy worrying about or addressing vision. In their minds, things were fine before the vision process, and things will be fine after it goes away. If they can just humor the pastor until the next compelling leadership technique comes along, they decide they won't have to think about "the vision thing."

Coexistence is often found in churches that are mid-size and over-programmed, and in congregations comprised of people who struggle with commitment because of their personal circumstances (e.g., high proportions of singles over 40 and divorced adults; highly transient communities).

Some Churches Accept the Vision

Some churches fare a bit better and gain overall *acceptance* of the vision. These congregations generally acknowledge the value of vision. They endorse the vision detailed for them by their church leaders, and they allow procedures to be implemented that could lead to the realization of the vision. They are, in essence, supportive of the vision, the visionary, and the practices related to vision. They are, however, not driven by the vision.

Often the problem is that these churches have never seen intense devotion to a life-changing ideal modeled for them within a ministry context. This kind of reaction is common in turnaround churches, in ministries serving mostly busters, in seeker-dominated churches and in those that consist of a working-class congregation. It is typical to find that the pastor is either a weak leader, an ineffective preacher or one who leads solely by command rather than by example.

Some Churches Own the Vision

At the uppermost point on the vision continuum are those Bodies that claim full *ownership* of the vision. They are enthusiastic advocates of the objectives described by the vision. My research shows that these are the churches to watch. They are recreating the shape of ministry in America.

Where is your church on this simple continuum? And what role are you playing in ensuring that God's vision is the centerpiece of the ministry decision-making apparatus? The answers to those questions are critical in the life and history of the Church in the United States.

LOOK AT THE LEADERS GOD CHOSE FOR HIS PEOPLE THROUGHOUT SCRIPTURE. OVERALL, THEY WERE NOT THE BEST OR THE BRIGHTEST, BUT THEY WERE QUALIFIED BECAUSE THEY WERE ATTUNED TO GOD.

A Pastor's Vision

Much of the ferment about vision revolves around the senior pastor. That person is usually the senior leader in the church—not always the primary preacher—but typically the dominant leader. Let me share three insights I've gleaned from working with pastors who are the visionary leaders of their churches.

Sometimes I encounter staff, members and senior pastors who are emotionally unsettled by the notion that the vision for the church is given to the senior pastor. They argue that God can work through anybody, regardless of that person's education, certification, experience, title or spiritual maturity.

God Looks for Leaders

The reality of church leadership, however, is that God does not entrust His people to those who are incapable of leading others. Seeking to lead without vision is akin to taking people on a walk through the forest in the dead of night without flashlights, maps, guides or other necessary navigational resources.

Look at the leaders God chose for His people throughout

Scripture. Overall, they were not the best or the brightest, but they were qualified because they were attuned to God. Invariably, each leader was surrounded by, and had an intimate professional relationship with, other qualified, godly people. The fact that they were leaders did not discount the perceived importance of their colleagues nor did it minimize the significance or role of the gifts and abilities contributed by their supporting cast.

To lead means that someone has to be in charge, someone must make the final decision, one person must be in front, providing the guidance for the pack. Leadership by committee is an oxymoron. In the best leadership teams, a leader among leaders emerges. That senior leader is the one who knows where the aggregation is going, what they corporately hope to create and how they will accomplish the objective. That person is your primary visionary.

In the church, the senior pastor is the person who, as the lead shepherd, is called to be so inseparable from God that he or she is capable of discerning after much prayer, study and discipline, the vision of God for the people he or she is responsible to lead.

God gave the vision to Moses, not Aaron; to David, not Jonathan; to Paul, not Barnabas; to Abraham, not Sarah or Lot. One of the most significant privileges of a leader of a group of believers is to determine the unique vision God has developed for that group and to convey it to the group for its edification and empowerment.

The Leader Will Lead

Can someone in the church, other than the senior pastor, initially receive the vision? Absolutely, but then the senior pastor is, in practice, not truly the leader of the church, but merely the figurehead who occupies a position of leadership without having the mantle of leadership.

If the church is absolutely certain that the person serving as senior pastor is the one God ordained to be the real leader of the church—not just its preacher or its spokesperson—the church should expect that person to be the visionary as well. That does not mean others on staff and in the Body have no role to play in identifying, articulating and implementing the vision. They all have significant roles. It does mean, however, that they are to assist in identifying the vision rather than to act as primary identifiers.

A second realization is that when a pastor leaves a church, the vision stays put. Why? Because the vision, if it is truly from God, is for the church, not the pastor. Indeed, all of us, pastors and laity, are meant to have God's vision for our personal lives and ministries. When a senior pastor departs, that person leaves with his or her per-

138

sonal vision; but the corporate vision remains the exclusive property of the church.

When the Pastor Leaves

The loss of a senior pastor has some complicated implications for ministry. For instance, if the vision stays behind after a senior pastor leaves, that vision should become the centerpiece of the pastoral search process. The church need not agonize about what kind of pastor it is seeking. The vision defines it. In short, the church is searching for a person who not only resonates with the people of the congregation, but who also possesses a ministry vision that is compatible with that of the church.

If a candidate for the position feels led to carry the church in another direction, chances are overwhelming that he or she is the wrong person for the job. Similarly, if a candidate evaluates the vision and finds that it does not fit as a comfortable shoe, that person should withdraw.

Suppose a pastoral change takes place. Does the incoming pastor bring a new vision for the church? In the vast majority of situations, absolutely not. The pastor is not the church. The pastor is the leader of the church, is responsible to God's vision for that part of the Body of Christ. The incoming pastor is responsible for reinforcing the core of the vision, for updating and refining the peripheral elements of the vision and for revisiting the strategic and tactical focus of the church. (In the next chapter, I will identify those rare instances when the vision needs to be changed. These, however, are the exceptional cases.)

Beware of Substitute Vision

Note one of the implications of an incoming pastor who redirects the vision of the church. Suddenly the church is wholly dependent upon the pastor. It will never fully mature as a Body of believers engaged in ministry, because the pastor is the charismatic centerpiece of the ministry. That pastor has substituted his or her vision for that of God.

The United States is littered with personality-driven churches in which the focal point of the ministry is accomplishing the objectives dictated by the senior pastor rather than by God's vision for the congregation. Often the pastor-initiated vision results in tremendous, beneficial ministry; but it is not the path God had chosen for the congregation. At some point, the church and those to whom the church could have ministered will suffer.

A final significant point. A visionary pastor stays put when ensconced in a ministry setting in which his or her gifts are used to the fullest, the vision is in synch with that of the church and the Body

139

is unified in its pursuit of the vision. Probably the most enthralling experience a visionary leader can have is to lead a group that owns the vision and exemplifies a full commitment to that vision. Because it is difficult for a church to become vision driven, once a senior pastor finds his or her niche, that person is loathe to leave it for another ministry assignment.

Backing Into the Vision

Another danger to avoid is that of backing into the vision. Some churches have weak leaders who are more interested in achieving vision that is derived from consensus among the people than through obedience to God.

Sadly, vision is treated as something that can almost be voted on in those churches. It is the most widely accepted understanding of the future based on human insight. The church does not seek God's mind for the future, but instead collects its own perspectives and formulates them into an agreeable package.

Why go this route? Usually because the pastor is not a mezzo-visionary and, therefore, is desperate to arrive at a notion of how the church can influence the community. The only reasonable solution to a person who is a micro-visionary in a mezzo-visionary role is to lean on others for intellectual and political support. Allowing the masses to dictate that future is then justified as God's way of using everyone's gifts.

Had Joshua, Josiah, David or Paul played to the masses and followed their desires, they would not be portrayed in the Bible as heroes of the faith, but rather as victims of their own weakness and folly.

A church backs into what it may call "vision" by seeking an immediate end to intense conflict, thus focusing on the future to deflect attention from the present pain and division. This, of course, has nothing to do with vision, but is simply a poor strategy for conflict management. Usually, after a period of time in which the alleged vision is pursued and shows little progress, the conflict becomes even more acrimonious.

The most common way of easing into a so-called vision is by examining what the church has been doing and by writing a vision statement that describes the existing activity, projecting a continuation of the current behavior and programs a few years hence.

The misfortune in this approach is that the result is not visionary. It projects a preferable future based on an accurate understanding of God, self and circumstances, but is survivalist in nature. This approach focuses on the past and present rather than on the future and typically calls for comfort and continuity at the expense of change. It most often coddles people rather than stretches them. The role of those in charge becomes caretaking rather than leading. The outcome is stability, not growth.

Why Leaders Stay Put

One of the benefits of having a visionary pastor is that it enables the church to retain visionary people. That may sound as if it is no big deal, but I have discovered that a church that lacks a visionary leader usually is unable to keep visionary people happy and productive.

A visionary pastor who encounters fellow visionaries rejoices in having other kindred spirits as partners in ministry. For the visionary, being surrounded by other visionaries makes life less predictable, but more exciting and productive. Far from being a threat, the visionary recognizes that other visionaries benefit rather than detract from the established order and structure.

Embracing the Vision-Led Christian

How Churches Respond to the Presence of Visionary Believers

The Visionary Church:	The Visionless Church:
Has a visionary pastor	Has a visionless pastor
Is excited by the presence of visionary individuals	Is threatened by the presence of visionary individuals
Listens for points of mutual interest	Demands compliance
Gives broad permission within the boundaries of the vision	Enforces restrictive parameters
Embraces the vision, then seeks the resources	Identifies its resources, then determines its options
Encourages people to pursue God's vision for their lives	Encourages people to focus on God's vision for the church
Rewards visionaries with more resources, responsibilities and opportunities	Seeks to control those who have vision

---

A Win-Win Result

Once a visionary pastor comprehends the visionary congregant, the task is to identify areas in which the person's vision matches that of the church. The effective church leader then releases the person to make the most of that particular aspect of vision.

In doing so, the visionary person gains a church home that values his or her ministry focus and efforts, and the church gains an activist whose energies will push the church closer to realizing its vision. This is one of all-too-rare circumstances in church work: the win-win situation.

Why is this process important? Because if the visionary senses that the church does not value the fundamental purpose of his or her existence, there is limited reason to believe that the church will provide a satisfying ministry base. It is the old "rich get richer" principle: Visionaries attract visionaries because they understand each other and appreciate the presence and intensity of other visionaries.

Professional church people (e.g., pastors, seminary professors, Christian journalists) are sometimes turned off by the energy level of churches such as Willow Creek or Saddleback Valley Community Church because they are vision-driven churches that attract visionary Christians, people of sharp focus, zealous nature and undeterred by the usual plethora of obstacles.

Intensity Is Scary

The intensity literally scares pastors and church people who come from visionless churches. I have heard from some people who shake their heads and compare vision-driven churches to cults. They misunderstand the passion, intensity and single-mindedness demonstrated in the congregations of these churches—qualities unlike those usually found in a so-called "real" church. The visionless have no frame of reference, so they interpret the visionary drive as compulsive and unnecessarily aggressive behavior that is unbiblical in character. The visionless just don't "get it."

If your church is vision led, vision driven and vision friendly, continue to build on that base of strength by identifying the points of mutual interest with other visionaries who come through the doors.

When Resistance Occurs

Why do some congregations accept God's vision and others fight it? One of the questions pastors who attend my vision seminar most often ask me concerns the unwillingness of their congregations to accept God's plan for the Body.

Most of the pastors who ask the question are convinced they have done their jobs of ascertaining and communicating the vision. "How can I get my people to buy into the vision?" they ask. "I have worked through the process and am confident that I know what God is calling us to. No matter how much I preach or teach about it, they don't seem to get it. What can I do?"

Some People Are Threatened

It is natural for people to resist vision. It poses a threat. It may be seen as God's imposition on their lives. It represents change and risk. It can be overwhelming. Many people, including good, godly, Bible-reading, praying, believing people, would rather continue along a known, if relatively insignificant path, than pursue a high-stakes, precise calling that demands their total commitment. In the tension between significance and security, some people choose the former, some choose the latter.

In many cases, I have discovered that people's objections were related to the inadequate conveyance of the vision to the congregation. The vision was *imposed* by the pastor, rather than organically developed so that it was jointly owned. Maybe it was preached about once, then ignored until the next year's "vision sermon" slot rolled around. Perhaps it was couched in such vague terms that people failed to understand. Often the vision is rejected because the leadership did not invest the time necessary to nurture the vision among the leaders before venturing into the congregation with that vision.

<u>143</u>

Communicating the Vision

The way the vision is communicated to the congregation is critical to its life in that Body. One of the most interesting aspects of my observations of how churches interact with God's vision is how leaders convey that vision to the people. Churches that possess a vision are those in which the vision is a constant focus, and in which the vision is communicated through a variety of media.

I find that the senior pastor plays a role by preaching about vision, in general; by teaching about the church's vision, in particular; by living in ways that are consistent with the vision and that make it overt to the congregation; by bringing attention to instances in which the church is living the vision; by meeting personally with people who need to know and embrace the vision; and by hiring staff and inviting people into leadership only if they give signs of truly owning the vision.

Other people in the church also play roles in heralding the vision. Leaders focus on it at retreats. They study how other churches have directed their visions. They expect the pastor, other leaders and the congregation at-large to be accountable to vision-consistent action. They evaluate the health of the church on the basis of the vision. They create plans, including goals and strategies, based on the vision.

They memorize the vision statement and use it in decision-making contexts. They remain enthusiastic about the vision as the focal point of their leadership activities.

Communicating the Vision

Unlimited Opportunities to Share the Vision:

- Sermons addressing the vision and the challenges facing the congregation.
- Personal vision casting and vision reinforcement meetings.
- Leadership retreats for discussing, praying about and creating strategies and plans regarding the vision.
- Teaching about mission, vision, values, goals, strategies, gifts, abilities and experiences.
- Exposing the people to case studies of how other people and ministries have handled vision.
- Calling attention to the church's existing vision-related activity and underscoring the successes.
- Including articles on vision in congregational communications.
- Relating every sermon or lesson to the church's vision.
- Incorporating vision as part of every training program the church provides for initiation, assimilation and leadership development.
- Hiring staff or promoting people to leadership positions only if they give evidence of embracing the vision.
- Key church leaders demonstrating the vision in daily pursuits.
- Posting the vision statement on all internal documents.
- Making the vision a core criteria in all decision-making efforts.
- Regularly reviewing the church's progress in relation to the vision.

Helping the Blind See

What are the options if reasonable efforts have been pursued and the congregation does not buy the vision? What can church leaders—senior pastor, staff, lay leaders—do to overcome the omnipresent objections to the pursuit of God's vision? The following are the most frequent remedies I have witnessed in churches as the means to satisfying people's concerns.

1. Create an environment conducive to vision. Most churches are not ready for vision. Remember what vision entails: change, risk, growth, innovation, passion, focus, courage and evaluation. These are uncomfortable attributes to introduce into any existing system of relationships and activity. They might be more threatening in a church than elsewhere because people often are allowed to become comfortable. They might fight tooth and nail against eliminating their comfort zone.

INSTITUTING VISION DEMANDS STRONG, EFFECTIVE LEADERSHIP. THE CHAMPION OF THE VISION MUST COURAGEOUSLY AND CONTINUALLY ASSERT NOT ONLY HIS OR HER LEADERSHIP, BUT MUST ALSO BASE IT ON THE CONTENT OF AND COMMITMENT TO THE VISION.

One of the most important and difficult tasks of the senior leader, therefore, is to prepare people by developing a climate that permits a vision's introduction. Once the appropriate alterations have been made, the stage is ready. Until that time, dissension, rejection and resentment are virtually guaranteed.

Frankly, another key is for the primary leader to inspire people. Vision is more than just a desirable objective. In the hands of a skilled leader, it is also an instrument of focus and motivation. If the vision does not inspire people, examine the vision. It might not be from God, it might not be communicated effectively or the people might be spiritually dead. The visionary should be able to build a ministry context in which the vision attracts interest, builds excitement, then stimulates participation.

2. The pastor must redefine the church's ministry so that it is consistent with, and driven by, the vision. Sometimes the power brokers or a group of renegades from within the congregation challenge the pastor to a game of chicken (i.e., they muster bold, intentional and coordinated resistance to the vision and wait to see who flinches first). Vision becomes the hot political issue because it is undermining their safety zones, perhaps even restructuring the power and authority base within the church.

Instituting vision demands strong, effective leadership. The champion of the vision must courageously and continually assert not only his or her leadership, but must also base it on the content of and commitment to the vision.

Members of the congregation need to comprehend that they are a Body in constant transition. God is eternally using different tools and instruments to shape His people. Vision is one of those means to His holy objectives. The embrace of His vision for the Body is crucial because it is the articulation of the heartbeat of the ministry. To be wholly and internally consistent, there is no backing away from the vision. This is one of those instances where the pastor must remain loving, firm, concerned and resolved.

Receiving God's vision is like being elected to the presidency: Once you've got it, there's no turning back.

3. Reinforce the principle that the vision is for the church, not the pastor. Many church attenders assume that when the vision is cast, it reflects the spiritual passions or personal whims of the pastor. If they are right, then you do, indeed, have problems. The vision is designed for the good of the Body, but is to be shepherded into reality by the pastor. It is not the pastor's vision, nor is it God's vision for the pastor. It is God's vision for the church.

Pastors rarely differentiate for the congregation their vision from God as opposed to God's vision for the Body. Helping people recognize the difference may, in itself, defuse concerns. Many people in the pews wonder what will happen to the church if the pastor leaves. Is the investment in the vision wasted because the vision presumably goes along with the pastor? To minimize the uproar caused by the introduction or renewed focus on vision, address such errant, but important, anxieties.

4. People must become insiders. People often object to vision because they have been left out of the process or because they assume that when the vision is in place they will be left out of the mainstream of the ministry.

Bringing people into the circle of owners is no simple or quick task. It takes more than a few sermons and an article in the church newsletter, although such inputs are certainly part of the process.

It takes many one-to-one meetings with staff and lay leaders. It requires small group meetings with core members of the congregation. It means staging special events that present a practical and inviting vision. Generating congregation-wide ownership of the vision is a long-term process that consumes substantial resources, but it is an investment that cannot be undervalued or shortchanged.

5. Involve people in the vision-development process. In my book *The Power of Vision,* I describe the role of the pastor and why he or she is the dominant visionary in the church. Recognize, though, that the pastor is to be a dominant, not a domineering player in this process. If you want to optimize the vision, involve people in the process from the start.

How? Be creative. Think about all the resources you would love to have at your disposal in discerning the vision and ask your people to help acquire those resources. Determining God's vision for your joint future is too important to approach without the necessary or desirable resources.

You might, for example, enlist a study group responsible for collecting, analyzing and presenting information about the ministry context: local demographics, community needs, lifestyle patterns, competition to the church and so forth. Involve people in conceptualizing and deploying a process for articulating the vision for the Body. Enlist the assistance of a few capable core leaders in the wording of the vision. Ask for a group to study the vision-building procedures and outcomes of other churches and to report its findings to the larger group. Establish a prayer vigil that upholds the pastor and the process.

Identify people's areas of giftedness and invite them to use their gifts in creative and meaningful ways in the overall campaign. Those gifted with hospitality could host vision-casting parties. Those gifted as teachers could lead Sunday School classes or small groups in a special series about vision. People gifted in giving could provide the seed money to launch a vision-based campaign.

Obtaining early and significant involvement in the process invariably helps the pastor come to grips with vision. This level of participation is especially useful in compensating for organizational structures that are based on committees, commissions and other groups that dictate the course of action within the church.

Anticipating the need to "go through the proper channels" without actually derailing the way God works is neither manipulative nor political. Involving people in substantive ways that help the pastor know the mind of God, without circumscribing the relationship of the pastor to God, benefits the entire Body.

6. *Each person must have a meaningful role in fulfilling the vision.* One of the baseline attractions of the church is that people want to belong to a family. If you have cast the vision without providing every person with a reasonable role, you have just cut them off from the family. It is not enough to explain the vision and to identify generic roles that people may pursue if they wish.

The most effective vision-based churches are those that have developed ways of personally communicating the vision to each person, and then incorporating everyone into the flow of ministry activity that emanates from the vision. This means going beyond comprehending the vision and delving into the actual distribution or assignment of functions in its implementation. Make sure your people feel

147

they own the vision. That happens when they have a significant, personal stake in it.

7. *Jettison your anchors.* Most of the churches I have studied that introduced vision experienced significant resistance. (The exceptions have been newly planted churches in which the vision was part of the birthright and a constitutional element, and thus was not susceptible for debate.) In every one of the congregations in which vision identification and vision casting created a ruckus, the resistance subsided after some of the actions previously described had been instituted.

In each case, some congregants remained stiff-necked and unyielding. The pastors had tried to work through the process with those people, but to no avail. Those people became the thorn in the side of the pastor and a nightmare for the entire leadership team of the church. What to do?

Addressing Challenges to Church Vision

1. Create an environment conducive to considering, discerning, owning and living the vision.
2. The pastor must exert strong leadership by redefining the church's ministry to be totally consistent with, and driven by, the vision.
3. Reinforce whom the vision is for: the church, not the pastor.
4. People must own the vision, which requires an investment of time and energy in comprehending it.
5. Involve people in the vision-development process.
6. Each person in the church must have the opportunity to assume a meaningful role in fulfilling the vision.
7. Cut loose your anchors.

Invite Dissidents to Leave
This may sound harsh, but follow the logic. Invite stubborn people to find a church home that suits them better. Don't portray them as enemies or ignorant or problematic. The reality is that this may be the first time anyone has clarified what the church stands for and where it is headed.

The reality dissidents hear may be different from the reality they have experienced. They may be fighting for something they thought they were getting when they came to the church. Your job is to help them make a decision, which is to get on board and sail in harmony with the rest of the crew or find a ship sailing to a destination they find amenable.

This may sound cold and heartless. It is not. If you allow these problem people to cling to your ship, I guarantee they will be anchors that drag down your expedition. They won't be happy, you won't be happy, the church won't be happy, visitors won't be happy. Nobody wins.

By helping dissidents find a place that meets their expectations and needs, everybody wins. Notice, I said you should help them find a new place of worship and community. Don't usher them out the back door, offering the right foot of fellowship. As their spiritual leader, you have a responsibility for their spiritual health. Take that duty seriously, even when it hurts.

Stick with It

Sometimes vision is little more than the latest fad that church leaders adhere to as a quick fix. They soon find, however, that a quick fix in ministry doesn't exist. If you want to grow, true spiritual development takes hard work, substantial resource investment and a long-term commitment. Ministry guarantees no sure thing or an easy win. We are engaged in an eternal life or eternal death battle with powers that dwarf our imaginations. Sometimes our best attempts to serve God meet with unexpected and potent resistance.

149

Providing Staying Power

A church might implement a few activities that enhance the staying power of the vision. Where appropriate, determine what might be done to increase the prospects for success.

• Most important of all, *the vision must truly be from God*. If it is human vision, it is destined to failure. If you find yourself in this situation, have the courage to acknowledge the reality; repent for your self-indulgence and focus on discerning and implementing God's vision.

• The vision must be *consistently reinforced* for the people. Bombarded with information, opportunities and challenges every day, in every walk of life, it is easy to forget the vision of one's church. We must make it easier for people to remember it and live it by continually reminding them in creative, appealing and meaningful ways.

• Congregations are attracted to success. They will not remain diligent in those things that are difficult and unproductive. If you have cast the vision and have been involved in its pursuit, *highlight the manifestations of vision-related progress*. Let people see the tangible fruits of the vision. Making a positive difference becomes self-reinforcing. An incremental victory a day keeps the evil one at bay.

• Leaders within the church cannot lose their *enthusiasm* for the vision. They must model long-term, fearless commitment. If their interests or commitments wane, the battle is lost.

• After a while, continue to *clarify the vision,* to explain how it is implemented and how is has influenced people's lives. The more experience the church has with the vision, the more real it should become.

• Sometimes vision becomes the heart of a power struggle. One or more people may seek to shift the focus of the church to embrace their preferences and desires. The effective visionary church learns how to *handle competing interests.* If these are visionaries, the leaders of the church will be able to mesh individual visions with the church's vision. If they are people who need attention, the church will minister to them without becoming sidetracked from its vision. If they are people whose vision is incompatible with that of the church, the church will help channel their passions and energies in effective ministries, which may be in nonchurch settings.

• The vision will make waves only if the church *creates systems that serve the vision.* Status quo churches often kill vision by insisting that the vision fit within archaic and ill-adapted structures. To thrive, a visionary church must be willing to design systems, structures and procedures that facilitate efficiently implementing the vision.

• *The congregation must continue to believe that it is capable of creating a better future on the strength of God's vision.* If that confidence dissipates, so will the backbone and resolve of the church, especially when it experiences hard times, such as environmental challenges, congregational disputes, leadership changes, resource shortfalls and cultural conflicts. Knowing that the vision represents a route to God's blessing toward realizing a livable and righteous world keeps people invested in that future perspective.

• One mark of a church in which the vision will live is the church's attitude toward change. Ministries flourish that intentionally focus on *identifying the next change point, and design mechanisms for maximizing such change.* Charles Handy speaks about this orientation in terms of implementing a continuing series of Sigmoid curves—instituting the next significant change before the last one has hits its peak, thus enabling the entity to stay on a comparatively unencumbered growth curve.[1]

God's vision, of course, never dies; but sometimes His people severely cripple it through their mishandling.

Providing Vision with Staying Power

- The vision must be from God.
- The vision must be consistently and convincingly reinforced.
- People must experience visible, tangible progress.
- Leaders must remain genuinely enthusiastic about the vision.
- The vision must become increasingly clear to a broader base of the church as time goes on.
- The church must respond appropriately to competing visions in its midst.
- Systems must be designed that facilitate efficiently implementing the vision.
- The people must persist in the belief that they can create the future.
- The church must press for constructive, constant change that corresponds with the visions of individuals.

Numbers Will Change

Here is another principle I have learned in studying vision. After you first articulate the church's vision, the number of people involved in the life of the church probably will decrease. The reason is that when people discover the church's character and intentions, they might also realize they are in the wrong place. Praise God for the clarity that vision gives to us all, enabling each of us to find the proper place for growth and service.

I also have learned that after the initial period of decline, and a short period of stability, the church usually recovers its prevision numbers and then surpasses those levels on the way to new numerical records. Why? Once the word spreads that your church stands for something, that it is wholeheartedly committed to something special and that people can be a part of it, those with whom the vision resonates will come running.

It is so unusual to find a church, or any institution, that is focused and effective. People are searching desperately for true leadership and for meaning in life. Offer people visionary leadership and well-defined significance wrapped in biblical truth, and you have an unbeatable package.

Note

1. Charles Handy, *The Empty Raincoat* (London: Arrow Books, 1994).

10

Turning Vision into Disaster

"IN THE ABSENCE OF A GREAT DREAM,
PETTINESS PREVAILS."
—PETER SENGE

Let's be candid. Vision is exciting, rewarding and life altering, but it is not easy to identify, articulate, implement or evaluate. Becoming involved with vision can sometimes lead to disaster.

Consider three major tension points for the individual or church in pursuing vision. First, let's determine if and when vision can be extinguished. Second, let's reflect on when it is appropriate to change the vision. Then, let's consider the reality of measuring progress to fulfill the vision.

Going, Going, Gone

Nothing is more pathetic than a church that catches "vision fever," loses it and becomes complacent. It reminds me of listening to Yankee baseball games on the radio when I was a boy. Occasionally, one of my heroes, such as Mickey Mantle or Yogi Berra, would come to the plate and hit a long drive to the outer reaches of the field.

The announcer would excitingly scream into the microphone, "It's well hit, it's heading for the fence, the right fielder is going back, back, back to the wall, he jumps, it's, it's...ooohhhh, he snared it just as it cleared the top of the fence, stealing a homer." In a couple of seconds, I would change from mild-mannered listener to excited fan, then back to the mild-mannered fan, or sometimes to a disgruntled, disappointed, less hopeful fan.

Church members who have confronted God's vision and have become excited and then lost their fervor for His direction are like the disappointed baseball fan. They go from inert observer to highly involved participant then back to inert observer, harder to motivate the next time the same possibility arises. Unlike the baseball fan who is listening to the game for diversion or entertainment, the stakes for the church or individual believer who loses the vision are much higher.

Do you remember companies such as RCA and F. W. Woolworth? They were two of the great consumer products giants of the past generation, but the companies are no longer of consequence. The lesson is that being a leader in the marketplace does not protect you from losing the vision in the course of time. Sometimes leadership might hasten decline by blinding the organization or individual to weaknesses and by creating a false sense of blessing and invincibility.

Why, then, do individuals or organizations that have God's vision driving them to greater heights sometimes lose the vision altogether? The answer lies in changes that occur relative to inputs, perspectives and conditions. To my surprise, the reasons are the same for individuals as for senior pastors and for churches. They may look a bit different in response to the divergent context of each, but the underlying effect is similar. Study the following 14 reasons people lose one of God's most precious gifts.

How Vision Is Lost

Neither individual believers, nor the visionary leaders of churches, nor congregations themselves are immune to the importance of nurturing. Unless the entity in question has a steady diet of positive nurturing, it will slowly lose its strength, then its focus, then its purpose.

Being Out of Touch with God
One instance of the nurturing need is for a visionary ministry unit (i.e., the believer, the leader or the congregation) to remain in *close*

communion with God. You have probably observed it before: A person or church that was once in love with God and fully devoted to His service begins to lose the focus on Him and eventually becomes Christian in name or reputation only. The heart has changed and, with it, the vision has faded away.

Stray from God and you can lose the vision. Is it because He takes it away from us or because we have unconsciously abandoned it? I don't know. It probably makes no difference. The principle remains true regardless of how it happens. Depart from God's presence, and His vision will depart from you.

Burnout

Sometimes you will find that a person or church loses the vision because of *burnout.* In a driven culture, in which we are better known for what we accomplish than who we become, Christians are as likely as other people to suffer the effects of flagging intensity. Lose your

> VISION IS A LONG-TERM APPROACH TO LIFE.
> IT IS NOT SOMETHING YOU WILL ACCOMPLISH IN
> THE NEXT QUARTER, THE NEXT YEAR AND PROBABLY
> NOT WITHIN THE NEXT DECADE.

155

passion, and your vision becomes just another responsibility you dutifully but joylessly lug around. The failure to receive regular refreshment and to constantly grow spiritually will rob you of the vision.

Poor Leadership

Similarly, some people give up on the vision because they have experienced *poor leadership* (i.e., people in positions of leadership who did not nurture the vision through instruction, encouragement, reinforcement, evaluation or other forms of assistance).

Visionaries need some form of leadership from other visionaries, whether it is teaching they glean from afar or from personal encouragement they receive nearby. The absence of leadership that promotes and propels the vision of a believer or a church can allow the focus of the visionary to go astray.

Absence of Accountability

In a similar vein, some people lose the vision because nobody has held them *accountable* for implementing it. Face it, at a base level, we all do only what we have to do. If nobody seems to care whether you implement the vision, why bother? Sure, for a while you may be self-regulating, but that conscientious behavior wears down in the face of multiple challenges and opportunities. Especially when an unseen spiritual foe pulls you in other directions.

Impatience

The most common way of losing vision is by losing perspective on reality. See if any of these alternatives strike a resonant chord within you.

Vision is a long-term approach to life. It is not something you will accomplish in the next quarter, the next year and probably not within the next decade. Of course, we are in a hurry. We don't have 2, 5, 10 or 20 years to invest. We need results now! If it can't be done quickly, our culture tells us, it is probably not worth doing.

If sociologists are correct in telling us that our culture is now reinventing itself every 3 to 5 years, a 20- to 30-year vision could, theoretically, be outdated and irrelevant several times before we see it fulfilled. The Japanese can teach us in this regard. They have a common perspective that if an organization will develop properly and enjoy long-term success, the secret is timing. They contend that building a great company takes 25 to 50 years!

That viewpoint is pertinent to our experience with vision. If it is from our everlasting God, the frenetic schedule many of us pursue has nothing to do with His eternal purposes and timetable. Our *impatience* to see the vision completed may cause us to lose interest, which then becomes the impetus that undermines the influence of that vision.

A Broadened Focus

A common weakness, especially in churches, is that once they pursue the vision and experience some initial successes with it, they then try to save the world and to embrace every opportunity that comes their way, regardless of the vision's *focus*. How many churches can you name that once were vibrant places of focused ministry but have evolved into large, lethargic, limp ministries because they now try to do everything for everybody?

These congregations transition from vision-led, purposeful churches into one-size-fits-all ministries that lose their characters and their qualities. Individuals can fall prey to the same paralysis.

Egocentricity

Sometimes people lose the vision because the success they have had with God's vision blurs their perception. They stop acknowledging that it is God blessing His vision and start to believe in their own abilities. *Egocentricity* can squelch God's spirit incredibly fast. Ministry

---

Lost: God's Vision.
What Causes It?

Input Problems:
1. Out-of-touch with God
2. Burnout
3. Poor leadership
4. Absence of accountability

Distorted Perspective:
5. Impatience
6. Broadening of focus
7. Egocentricity
8. Ignoring values
9. Seduced by other visions, interests
10. Ministry becomes tedious
11. No evaluation of vision progress

Injurious Conditions:
12. Inappropriate structures/lifestyle
13. Extreme conflict
14. The vision becomes outdated

---

becomes a means to glorifying self rather than God, so the vision He provided takes a backseat to the evolving vision emanating from the minister.

Ignoring Values

Values, which serve as a foundation for developing and exercising God's vision, are occasionally the problem. Take away your values and implementing your vision is an empty set of motions, doing good for the sake of doing good. That kind of vapid activity cannot endure for long.

Another Vision or Other Interests

Some individuals or ministries lose the vision when competing objectives seem more significant. Satan is a wily one. It is possible to convince a believer or an entire congregation of believers that outcomes other than God's vision are the most important results to seek. The lure might be the rewards accruing to those who achieve such objectives (money, reputation, fame, opportunities), or it might be the emotional comfort realized by pursuing those objectives. Whatever the bait, once hooked on *another vision or interest*, everyone is cheated out of the best possible results.

Ministry Becomes Tedious

A surprising number of Christians lose the vision because the long, hard road toward achieving victory simply becomes a chore. For the pastor, leading the people *becomes tedious*. For the believer, living the Christian life becomes a series of stilted rituals and traditions. For the congregation, Sunday is a time to play church and go through the motions. The passion, which once burned bright, turns into cold, gray ashes.

Lack of Evaluation

Another reason related to the loss of vision and the distortion of perspective is the *lack of evaluating* the progress of the vision. Unless an

BECAUSE CHURCHES AND PEOPLE
PREFER COMFORT TO PAIN, AT TIMES WE INSTITUTE
LIFE CHANGES INTENDED TO RESOLVE OR
TO MITIGATE CONFLICT.

ongoing means exists for evaluating your vision quest, you have little reason to feel excited. After all, possessing vision is one thing; converting it into profound, life-changing outcomes is something else. Thus, without a yardstick, it is hard to maintain the enthusiasm for the calling.

Inappropriate Structures and Lifestyles

Certain conditions contribute to the vision's impairment. One relates to a church's *organizational structure*. It might be the kinds of programs that exist; it might be the staff roles that are or are not filled; it might be the policies that limit risks; it might relate to the restrictions placed on the church by facilities or by a denomination.

For individuals, the question is one of *lifestyle,* including relationships, career, family and finances. Any or a combination of these factors may limit what the individual is able or is willing to do to turn vision into action. If the limitations for the individual or church become too monolithic, a decision must be made: whether to change the structures or lifestyle or to deprioritize the vision. The latter choice generally has disastrous ministry consequences.

Extreme Conflict
Another circumstantial consideration is the existence of *extreme conflict* in the life of the visionary. The presence of conflict may refocus the energy of the visionary to things other than the vision. Because churches and people prefer comfort to pain, at times we institute life changes intended to resolve or to mitigate conflict.

The Vision Becomes Outdated
If those changes have the desired effect, we continue them, and perhaps upgrade the intensity with which we implement those steps. One consequence is often reordering our priorities in life. When this happens, the vision that had defined us prior to the conflict may seem as if it is an inconvenience or a minor diversion because of the ability we now have to sedate ourselves to potentially painful or harmful conflicts. The least common of the reasons for losing the vision is that the vision, though faithfully pursued, *has become outdated.*

159

Out with the Old

Earlier I noted that vision runs on a long-term track and that it often outlives the visionary. On occasion, however, it may be appropriate to reevaluate the vision and to seek a new vision from the Lord.

I discuss this possibility with some hesitation. The hesitation is based on firsthand experience with churches that are constantly looking for a window of opportunity to change the vision because of a need to alleviate the pressure of engaging in life-changing ministry.

If they can make a transition to a different vision, the time devoted to discerning that vision and then to strategizing for its fulfillment buys them time to relax while holding on to the hope that the new vision will be more comforting and comfortable.

Knowing that a vision can be fulfilled, or that circumstances merit revisioning, offers some people or churches an escape clause of sorts. Yet, it would be misleading to ignore discussing those times when you may legitimately seek a new vision.

In Search of a New Vision
I know of only five instances when it seems viable to redetermine the vision:

1. When *substantial change* occurs in the demographic character of the community in which a church or an individual ministers. This does not mean that vision is about demographics. More often than not, vision has less to do with the characteristics of the recipient audience than it has to do with the results that are to be achieved. If the players change, however, the game may change as well.

2. Similarly, *if a church dies*, either because it has few remaining people or because the remaining people are vision bankrupt, it may be time for a new vision to resuscitate the ministry. The equivalent circumstance for an individual is if he or she experiences dramatic change in family, particularly divorce, death of a spouse or the point at which all of the children are no longer living in the home or in the care of their parents.

3. *When a church changes pastors.* This might be a reason to expect that a new vision would come with the pastor; although this is primarily true in cases where the incoming pastor is the first to truly cast God's vision for the church or where the new leader is replacing a long-term visionary and the vision had been largely accomplished.

4. When the church or individual is certain that the vision in which it has been operating was *human, not God given.*

5. *When the vision has been fulfilled.*

If you encounter any of these scenarios, it is time to go back into the Word, back on your knees, start fasting and gather all the godly counsel you can to discern where God is leading you.

Short of these conditions, however, I encourage you not to give up too quickly on the vision God already has provided. He is patient and long-suffering. Try to match His patience and perseverance. Discarding His unfinished vision is an act of disobedience and will lead you to a fruitless chase for new vision when the old vision is still relevant and necessary.

Measuring the Vision's Progress

Without some kind of reliable measurement process to determine whether you are remaining true to the vision, it is easy to get off track. I have observed example after example of people and churches failing to evaluate their vision quest, resulting in effort after effort that moves them farther from fulfilling their vision.

This wayward action results when no standards or means of correction exists. Thus, at the crucial time when they believed they were visionaries in action, they were acting in opposition to their vision, actually making it harder to accomplish the specific objectives they had set out to achieve. A simple mid-course evaluation could have alerted them to the fact that they were traveling on the wrong track.

Vision supports three primary components, each of which is measurable. Each of those components—comprehension, ownership and impact—relate to specific behaviors. The forms of measurement you use will, by necessity, vary in nature and in reliability. I suggest you consider a mixture of quantitative (i.e., statistical) and qualitative (i.e., nonstatistical) measures.

Measure Comprehension

Of the three dimensions you might study, comprehension is probably the most difficult to measure. Vision comprehension means evaluating how well you understand the vision. No absolute standard is available for this assessment. The examination will be subjective.

What indicators might help you recognize how well you comprehend your vision? Generally, you will have to rely upon measures of retrospective knowledge of opportunities and how completely you

> CHANCES ARE, IF YOU CANNOT TRANSLATE YOUR
> VISION INTO SUCCINCT AND COMPELLING STATEMENTS
> TO THOSE WITH WHOM YOU WORK OR INTERACT, YOU
> ARE UNCERTAIN ABOUT ITS CONTOURS.

161

exploited those opportunities. If, for instance, you look at the past six months and can identify 10 situations you ignored, but that could have afforded chances to implement your vision, you have an indication that perhaps you do not fully comprehend the breadth of your vision.

You can probably detect the hole in this path of exploration, though. Most of us are neither very reflective nor analytical, so the chances of us having a fine-tuned sensitivity to our opportunities in life and how well we have exploited those options is not high.

The best option is to consider this aspect of your vision quest with the help of accountability partners. Enlist them to engage in such a review with you. Trusted, informed, caring associates may have a better grip on opportunities left untouched and be able to encourage your successes in taking advantage of various choices.

Another way of examining your comprehension is to study the decisions you have made in the recent past. Ask yourself about the role of your vision. For each of the decisions in question, how central a role did your vision play in your ruminations? In retrospect, how could you have decided differently to be more in tune with your vision?

You also might choose to evaluate how well you communicate your vision to others during the course of your travails. Chances are, if you cannot translate your vision into succinct and compelling statements to those with whom you work or interact, you are uncertain about its contours.

Further, you might consider how insightfully you have explored the points where your vision matches that of your church, of your mate and loved ones, of your place of work, of your colleagues at work and in ministry and of other high-profile leaders. People who do not seek those commonalties typically suffer from either low comprehension of their vision or from minimal ownership.

Measure Ownership

Vision ownership is a bit easier to measure. Your goal in this exercise is to determine your level of passion and commitment to the vision. This may be accomplished by answering questions such as the following:

- How often do you turn to your vision when making time management or purpose-related decisions? How satisfied are you with your decisions in terms of their ultimate consistency with your vision? Have they facilitated vision-consistent results or have they produced unrelated outcomes?
- Name the instances when you were confronted with good opportunities but you rejected them because they were inconsistent with your vision.
- How many hours a week do you devote to refining, enacting and examining your vision? Is the pattern one in which you are declining, consistent, increasing or unpredictable in the level of resources you commit to your vision?
- When you talk to people about the future, are you optimistic that you can make a difference? As you think privately about your future endeavors, do you become excited or discouraged about the future and about how you may influence it?
- When you meet new people and go through the introductory phase of the relationship, do you describe yourself and your life in terms of your vision?
- When people have conflicting goals, interests or plans,

how protective are you of your vision? How often do you find yourself giving in and doing things that are antithetical to your vision?

- On a subjective scale, how would you compare the intensity of confidence you have in your vision today with that which you had when the vision initially became clear to you?

Measure Impact

Vision impact may be the easiest to assess. The bottom line is identifying change that can be related to how you apply your vision. If you have experienced the typical planning process to integrate your vision into practical action, then examine your goals and determine how well you are doing at reaching the desired outcomes.

Invite a trusted and capable colleague to review your strategies and to determine whether they are geared to reaching your goals. More subjectively, take a look at your internal and external environments and determine whether they have changed during the past year and how much of that change can be attributed to your positive obsession with your vision?

163

Instruments of Insight

The methods and tools you use to collect information about your vision performance will vary. Be creative. There is no standard or right way to do this, and you are not trying to serve anyone other than yourself and God.

If you are evaluating how well your church is doing in its vision quest, a variety of data sources can be mustered. For instance, you could:

- Invite appropriate audiences to rate the church in specific vision-driven activities.
- Collect information from people in the church through informal conversations about what they experience at the church and through its ministries.
- Observe the transactions and interactions in meetings.
- Generate a regular series of statistics that measure formal outgrowths of vision activity (e.g. number of volunteers, volunteer hours, enrollment in gift assessment classes).
- Invite program leaders to conduct their own directed assessment of the relationship between their ministries and the church's (and their program's) vision.

- Conduct a formal review of progress toward specified goals.
- Count the times when the vision is publicly mentioned or alluded to, e.g. in sermons, in testimonies, in program descriptions, in budgeting negotiations, in performance reviews.
- Seek God's response through prayer.

A Personal Evaluation

If you are trying to determine how well you are doing in implementing your personal vision, you might turn to somewhat different avenues of evaluation, including the following:

- Create a self-evaluation survey you regularly complete and compare to see how you fare and if you are making progress.
- Seek honest feedback from accountability partners.
- Examine your calendar to see what effect your vision is having on how you allocate your time.
- Examine your checkbook to see what difference your vision makes in spending your money.
- Reflect on your decision-making process and how vision driven it is. What are the major considerations you lean on each time you have to make a moral, ethical, time-related or directional decision?
- Examine your goals to see if you are achieving them.

Take these measurements seriously. Write them down. Track them from year to year. Take each component and determine how you can upgrade your performance in that dimension so your next evaluation will show even better results. The sole purpose of the measurement process is to facilitate a life that is vision led and that is life transforming for the sake of Jesus Christ. Examine your results in view of this objective.

An old business adage warns: "If you can't measure it, it's not worth doing." Pursuing your vision is definitely worth doing. Make certain you invest resources in examining how well you are doing in your vision quest.

Creating the Future

"WHAT COULD BE WORSE THAN BEING
BORN WITHOUT SIGHT? BEING BORN
WITH SIGHT AND NO VISION."
—HELEN KELLER

These are turbulent times for the United States. Change is occurring faster than ever before, and many of the changes are profound. People are seeking perspectives that will help them navigate the rough waters of this change. They are seeking individuals who see the big picture and can help clarify where things are headed and how to make the most of the burgeoning opportunities.

Americans are actively searching for leaders who have confidence in something other than themselves and who can motivate others based on that faith.

In Search of Vision

Americans are crying out for vision.

We have tried the vision of political leaders and have found it disappointing. We have tried the vision of religious gurus and have found it distorted. We have tried the vision of major league business developers and have found it to be empty. We have tried the vision offered by philosophers and educators and have found it to be flawed.

> All a man's ways seem innocent to him, but motives are weighed by the Lord (Prov. 16:2).

Americans are crying out for God's vision.

What will our future be? No one knows for certain. We do know, however, that the future is being created, right now, by people who are driven by vision they believe in wholeheartedly, vision that others are willing to commit to, vision that they contend represents the best future for which we could hope.

We know that many, if not most, of the visionaries who are charging full steam ahead are not leading us down the path dictated by God, but are pursuing the whims and ideals they have concocted in their own minds or hearts.

> "For my thoughts are not your thoughts, neither are your ways my ways" declares the Lord (Isa. 55:8).

A Field Ripe for Harvest

Conditions are right for the Christian Body to reassert its leadership in our nation. Recapturing a position of influence has nothing to do with arresting political power or with flaunting numerical proliferation. It is based on the fundamental need to be loved by and in touch with God. It is based on the need for a life that has meaning and purpose, one that is driven and defined by things that matter.

The time is right for God's people to promote God's vision to produce God's objectives with God's blessings.

> "Write the vision and make it plain....For the vision is yet for an appointed time; but at the end it will speak, it will not lie" (Hab. 2:2,3, *NKJV*).

Where Do You Stand?

Where do you stand in the midst of this battlefield of ideas, beliefs, relationships, opportunities and visions? Let me ask you six closing questions.

1. Where do you stand on the vision hierarchy? Have you reached your maximum potential? If not, what are you doing to ensure that you reach that point?

2. Because every one of us who loves and trusts God is entrusted with at least micro-vision, how are you fulfilling that vision in your family, your career, your personal relationships and your church?

3. What is the vision of your church? At what points does your personal vision match those of your church? How persistent are you in blending God's vision for your life with that which He has given to your church?

4. As you encounter other people, how adequately do you discern their vision for life? For those people who need to grow in their vision, what steps do you pursue to support their development as visionaries?

5. What kind of results do you see emanating from your pursuit of God's vision? Who holds you accountable to the vision? What are the key measures you use for objective evaluation?

6. What evidence is there that you have fully embraced the vision, resulting in your thinking and behaving as a visionary would? How evident is the difference between your thinking and behavior today and that before you discerned God's vision?

No Substitute for Vision

If you wish to be a leader in any walk of life, at any level of sophistication or intensity, vision is a requirement. Nothing substitutes for God's vision—not hard work, extreme intelligence, clever ideas or lofty titles.

Your life counts to God. It can also count to other people whom God wants to influence through you if you seek, discern, own and fulfill His vision for you. Once you live by vision, you will never look back. Your life and the lives of those with whom you come in contact through implementing the vision will be utterly transformed. Praise God!

The Integrated Life

For vision to have its optimal effect, a person must coordinate his or her mission, vision, values, gifts, talents and experiences. The failure to connect these components leads to unnecessary barriers to influence, or to personal frustration. People who unify these elements derive greater joy and fulfillment from life. The following examples show how several people have put it all together into a package of perspective and performance, enabling them to maximize their daily existence for Christ.

How would you describe your mission, vision, values, gifts and talents?

Personal description: male, 41, married, two children.
Mission: to know, love and serve God with all my heart, mind and soul.
Vision: to interpret the culture and communicate the outcomes in ways that will facilitate people to develop a biblical worldview; to identify, develop, deploy and support true leaders; and to help create culturally relevant and biblically pure forms of the true Church of Christ.
Values: glorifying Christ, obedience to the vision, family fulfillment, serving others, self-acceptance, truth, hard work, stewardship, personal growth, acceptance, personal spiritual renewal.
Gifts: prophecy, teaching.
Talents: writing, public speaking, information analysis, logic, music.
Occupation: author.

Personal description: female, 40, married, two children.
Mission: to live like Christ at all times, in all situations, regardless of the cost.
Vision: to support my husband in his ministry endeavors by providing encouragement, honest evaluation and administrative assistance; and to raise our children to be believers in Christ, whose profession of faith is consistent with their behavior, values, attitudes and relationships.
Values: loyalty, honesty, enjoyment of life, loving relationships, wide range of experiences, respect for others, sacrifice, global consciousness.
Gifts: teaching, administration.
Talents: planning, organization, teaching.
Occupation: mother, homemaker.

Personal description: female, 31, married, one child.
Mission: to love God and to love others as myself.
Vision: to establish my home as a neighborhood center of care, compassion and emotional healing based on genuine relationships.
Values: love, hope, honesty, understanding, permanence, balance, acceptance, spiritual depth, community.
Gifts: mercy, hospitality.
Talents: cooking, crafts, child care, networking, homemaking, great memory.
Occupation: licensed in-home child-care provider.

Personal description: male, 55, single, no children.
Mission: to live in ways that bring glory and honor to God.
Vision: to create a global electronic network that permits effective dissemination of biblical knowledge to under-resourced believers and that delivers effective transmission of the gospel to nonbelievers.
Values: integrity, hard work, compassion, practical Bible knowledge, effective ministry, asceticism, commitment, simplicity.
Gifts: serving.
Talents: electronics, musical performance, craftsmanship.
Occupation: computer technician.

Personal description: male, 48, remarried, four children.
Mission: to receive God's blessings with humility and gratitude, and to bless others in return.
Vision: to restore hope and purpose to the lives of disadvantaged children through teaching Christ's love and practical life skills.

Values: justice, diversity, empowerment, personal dignity, encouragement, community, humility, sacrifice.
Gifts: mercy.
Talents: networking, counseling, negotiating, making people feel comfortable.
Occupation: public school teacher.

APPENDIX

2

Resources Regarding Mission, Vision, Values and Personal Composure

Abrahams, Jeffrey. *The Mission Statement Book*. Berkeley, Calif.: Ten Speed Press, 1995.

Anderson, Leith. *Winning the Values War*. Minneapolis: Bethany House Publishers, 1994.

Barker, Joel. *Future Edge*. New York: William Morrow & Company, 1992.

Barna, George. *The Power of Vision*. Ventura, Calif.: Regal Books, 1992.

Hedges, Charlie. *Getting the Right Things Right*. Sisters, Oreg.: Questar Publishers, 1996.

Hybels, Lynne and Bill. *Rediscovering the Church*. Grand Rapids: HarperCollins/Zondervan, 1995.

Kawasaki, Guy. *Selling the Dream*. New York: HarperCollins, 1991.

Lewis, Hunter. *A Question of Values*. San Francisco: Harper-SanFrancisco, 1990.

Liebig, James. *Merchants of Vision*. San Francisco: Berrett-Koehler, 1994.

Malphurs, Aubrey. *Developing a Vision for Ministry*. Grand Rapids: Baker Book House, 1992.

Nanus, Burt. *Visionary Leadership*. San Francisco: Jossey-Bass, 1992.

Senge, Peter. *The Fifth Discipline*. New York: Doubleday Currency, 1990.

Information About the Barna Research Group, Ltd.

The vision of the Barna Research Group, Ltd. is:

> To provide current, accurate and reliable information, available in bite-size pieces and at affordable prices, to church leaders for the purpose of facilitating better ministry decisions.

It took several years in business and struggling with God before this vision for the company became clear to George Barna. The emergence of this vision led to a comprehensive reengineering of the organization, and a shift in focus from serving major secular corporations to serving the local church. Although the way the vision is communicated has been modified since it was initially ascertained, the core elements of the vision have remained intact, and have determined the character and focus of Barna Research.

Since its beginnings in 1984, Barna Research has served more than 200 organizations. Some of its better-known clients have included Visa, The Disney Channel, Southwestern Bell Telephone, the U.S.

Army, CARE, United Cerebral Palsy and BankOne.

Among the many ministries served have been the Billy Graham Evangelistic Association, Campus Crusade for Christ, World Vision, Word Publishing, Thomas Nelson Publishing, American Bible Society, Prison Fellowship, Youth for Christ, Salvation Army, Willow Creek Community Church, Compassion International, Fuller Theological Seminary, Dallas Theological Seminary, Trinity Broadcasting Network, Ministries Today, New Man and many others.

Through its nationwide surveys, Barna Research explores the character, perspectives and behavior of the American people, especially in relation to their religious beliefs and faith experiences. The company is an independent, privately owned corporation dedicated to helping individuals, ministries and for-profit organizations that seek to enhance the quality of people's spiritual development.

Through the writings of the company president, George Barna, the company disseminates information through a wide variety of media. Among those are a bimonthly newsletter—The Barna Report—topical reports, audiotapes, live presentations of survey findings in seminars and conferences, videotapes and press releases. Barna has also written 21 books, including the following:

176

The Frog in the Kettle	*The Index of Leading Spiritual*
User Friendly Churches	*Indicators*
The Power of Vision	*Evangelism That Works*
Virtual America	*Generation Next*
Today's Pastors	*Turnaround Churches*
Church Marketing	*Absolute Confusion*
Baby Busters	*If Things Are So Good, Why Do I*
Ten Years Later	*Feel So Bad?*

For additional information about the Barna Research Group or available resources, please write to them at:

Barna Research
2487 Ivory Way
Oxnard, CA 93030

More Informative Resources from George Barna.

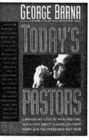
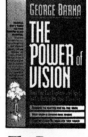

Resources from Elmer Towns

Continuing Education for Church Leaders.

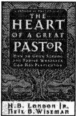

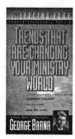
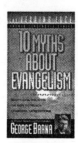